Before the Incas

Archaeological Sites of Coastal Peru

3rd Edition

Tommie Sue Montgomery

Before the Incas

Archaeological Sites of Coastal Peru

3rd Edition

Table of Contents

Acknowledgments

No book is the product of a singular effort, although writing is, of necessity, a solitary enterprise. This guide exists because many people, most of them Peruvian, have shared their knowledge and enthusiasm as my husband and I trekked around these—and many other—sites in Peru over the last 14 years. Several names are unfortunately forgotten but Victor at El Brujo, Dennis in Trujillo, Lorena at the Huaca de la Luna, Roosevelt at Caral, Freddy at Purucucho and Cajamarquilla, Victor at Mateo Salado, Alexander Astete at Vichama, Miguel Romero Baldeón at Bandurria, and Susie Cancho Aragonez in Nasca are memorable.

Carlos Palma, travel agent extraordinaire, made our first trip to Machu Picchu and Cusco unforgettable in 2010 and arranged many of the tours recounted herein. His company on the days we visited Purucucho and Cajamarquilla, then later Nasca and Ica, made those experiences particularly special. Esther Gorriti took time out of her busy schedule in 2009 to show us Pachacamac for the first time. Segundo Calderon Navarro, our go-to driver during our many trips to Lima, increased our pleasure on our long drives to Vichama, Bandurria, and other sites over the last 15 years with his knowledge of locales and great restaurants.

Several people read all or part of the first edition manuscript, found the inevitable typos, and contributed substantively to the text. A special thanks to Beth Blaney of Honolulu for reading an early draft and to Cate Green of Sydney, Australia, for catching later errors in the first two editions. David Abrahams, proofread the second edition. Un mil gracias to *limeños* Galia Gorriti and Professor Pedro G. Vásquez Ruesta for reviewing the entire manuscript. Rich Vecchio, of Fertur Travel in Lima, whose excellent articles I encountered on the Internet, permitted me to use the Moche creation story, and later agreed to read the entire manuscript. Rick suggested several additions, all of which have found their way into the text.

Finally, this project wouldn't have been nearly as much fun without my better half, my husband David Abrahams. Thanks for coming along!

Oshawa, Ontario

December 2023

The Palpa Geogliphs are associated with the Paracas Culture (600-200 BCE). There are at least 1600 lines and geoglyphs spread over the desert 141 km (84 mi) southeast of the Paracas Peninsula and north of the Nasca Lines, many of which have been discovered by drones—a new tool in the archaeologist's kit.

The most typical motifs are anthropomorphic figures with ray-like or feathered headdresses but there are also mythical figures and zoomorphic motifs of birds, monkeys, and felines. The geoglyphs are generally found on the top of ridges and sides of hills—like the "astronaut" among the Nasca lines. The geoglyphs in this image are just off the Pan American Highway about 14 km (8.5mi) north of the Maria Reiche Museum or 7 km (4 mi) south of the town of Palpa on the west side of the highway.

Preface

As I was leaving the showroom on Holland-America's Prinsendam in January 2017, after giving a lecture on pre-Inca civilizations in Peru, a guest stopped me. He said he wished that I had a book on the subject—a companion book to my just-published *Navigating Machu Picchu,* which was on sale in the ship's store. I had been thinking about it for a couple of years and his prod was the proverbial kick-in-the arse that I needed to begin putting this book together.

Conversations about pre-Columbian sites in Peru always begin—and often end—with Machu Picchu. While unquestionably the (supply your own superlative) must-visit site in Latin America, Peru has at least 80 extraordinary and memorable indigenous civilizations whose centres take us back in history more than 5,000 years. Many were spread over vast areas; for example, by the early 1960s, almost 700 archaeological sites dating from the late glacial period to the nineteenth century had been identified in central Peru alone.[1]

The first edition covered 12 sites that stretch from the coast north of Trujillo to south of Paracas. The second edition added three sites in Nasca along with two more that pre- and post-date Caral—until 2017 considered the oldest urban civilization in the Americas. Still, these 16 sites are not, by any stretch, exhaustive; there are numerous other civilizations and cultures from Ecuador to Chile and in the *altiplano*—the Andes—from where the Incas ultimately ruled.

A brief history of each civilization introduces it and all are sites that I have visited on at least one occasion, taking pictures and notes. The book is organized geographically from north to south, except for Bandurria, Caral-Supe, and Vichama. For several decades, Caral was identified as the oldest urban

---

[1] Patterson, T.C. & Moseley, M.E. Late Preceramic and Early Ceramic Cultures of the Central Coast of Peru. p. 115. http://digitalassets.lib.berkeley.edu/ anthpubs/ucb/text/nap006-007.pdf

civilization in the Americas; then artifacts at Bandurria were radiocarbon-dated and confirmed that it is 1,000 years older than Caral. In addition, the Chimú, Moche, Lima, Ischma, and Nasca Cultures are covered. Information to assist you in planning a visit is also included along with a list of suggested readings and a list of useful Spanish phrases. Throughout the book and at the end, you will find blank pages for your own notes.

A balsillo (tup) on the beach at Huanchaco, near Trujillo. This reed watercraft has been used by fishermen for at least 3,000 years and appears on Moche ceramics. They are made from the same reeds (Schoenoplectus californicus subsp. tatora) used to build the floating Uros Islands in Lake Titicaca—clear evidence of early Andean-coastal interchange. The Spanish named them "caballito de tortora" (little reed boat) because the fisherman straddles the boat while paddling.

General Information

1. The exchange rate for the Peruvian Sol and U.S. dollar, as of 26 December 2023, was S/3.68:US$1.00. Do NOT assume that U.S. dollars are accepted. While they are accepted at some places in Lima, such as the artisan markets and by hotel taxi drivers, entry fees must be paid in Peruvian Soles or with a credit card. Debit/Visa cards are usually but not always accepted. Outside Lima, few places or individuals will accept dollars. U.S. bills must be in mint condition to exchange; the slightest tear will cause a vendor to reject a bill because their bank will not accept it.

2. **Guides.** The great majority of guides at archaeological sites in Peru are university-trained and licenced by the Ministry of External Commerce and Tourism (MINCETUR). Most speak English as well as Spanish and, especially in the highlands, Quechua (in Cusco and the Sacred Valley) and Aymara (around Lake Titicaca).

3. **Tipping.** If you arrive at a site on your own there will be tour guides to lead you through the site and explain what you are seeing. Most sites require that you use a guide and many do not charge for this service; the guides everywhere except Bandurria are paid by the state or, in the case of El Brujo, the Weise Foundation, which operates the site in cooperation with the Peruvian government. In March 2018, the guides at Bandurria were paid only by entry fees and materials sold at the entrance. Because their salaries are far from North American or European standards, tipping at the end of a tour is usually warranted and always welcome.

4. All the sites in this book are located in deserts. They are hot and dusty. Wear comfortable walking shoes, hats, use sun screen, and take a water bottle.

5. **Do NOT take food into any site.** Bottled water is acceptable; just take your bottle with you when you leave!

6. **The meaning of *Huaca*.** Several of the site names in Trujillo and Lima begin with *Huaca*. In the Quechua language, *Huaca* is an object related to veneration and ritual, something revered. It is often a pyramid but can also refer to natural locations, such as enormous rocks.

7. **Taxis in Lima.** Every medium to large hotel has a few taxis that operate from the hotel. They are always black, unmarked, and the drivers' "uniform" is black pants and a dress shirt, usually white. There are also taxi stands at various locations throughout the city. Unless you speak Spanish and can give the driver clear directions, use one of these options; do not hail a cab—even a licenced cab—on the street. And, ALWAYS negotiate the price—by the hour or total cost for a trip, before getting in the taxi. Currently, hotel *taxistas* charge S/45-50 per hour, which is quite reasonable, especially given the cost of gasoline in Peru (about US$5.00 per gallon).

8. Apps like Uber, TaxiBeat, and EasyTaxi are also now available and widely used in Lima. If you have them on your smartphone, either with roaming data or an Internet connection, they will work. However, if you don't speak Spanish, you may have difficulty communicating with the driver.

9. **Cruise ship visitors**

a. **Lima.** Because the Port of Callao (where all cruise ships dock) is a working container port—one of the largest in Latin America—no one can walk around the port area. If you are on a ship's tour, the buses pick you up and deliver you back to the ship's side. If you are going off on your own, find out ahead of time where shuttle buses will drop you. The large shuttle buses run to one point in Lima: in front of the Marriott Hotel in Miraflores, which faces Larco Mar mall (built into the side of the cliff) and is a 30-40 minute ride from the port. From here it is 14 blocks to the centre of Miraflores, the Parque Kennedy. There is also a large taxi stand across from the Marriott; the drivers are all licenced.

If leaving the port on your own, be sure not to wander out into the streets of Callao and *never* have a taxi driver leave you at the main port entrance, where you will have to stand and wait for the next, returning shuttle to arrive. Robberies in this general area of Callao are common.

b. **Trujillo.** Cruise ships dock at the port of Salaverry, about 25 minutes south of Trujillo. There is nothing here and you cannot walk in the port area except to the area where vendors have set up kiosks with Peruvian handcrafts, most of which are not from the area. Taxi drivers, some with sedans, a few with minivans, are allowed into the port. You can arrange with them for a tour of the city of Trujillo, the various archaeological sites, or Huanchaco, the seaside town 15 minutes west of Trujillo where fishermen still go out on *balsillos* or *tup* (reed boats) just as their ancestors did two millennia ago.

c. **Paracas (Puerto San Martin).** If you have purchased tickets to fly over the Nasca lines from Pisco—the nearest airport—during your day in Paracas, you can arrange for transportation to and from the airport online. Or you can walk off the ship and negotiate with one of several taxi drivers to take you to the airport, wait for you, and then return you to the ship, perhaps with a stop in the seaside town of Paracas, which is worth a visit, or a tour of the Paracas Peninsula. If your ship is in port until 17:00, there is plenty of time to do one or the other. If you want to visit the Ballestas Islands (aka the Peruvian Galápagos) for far less than the ship's tour, take the shuttle bus into Paracas. It will let you off in front of the *Marina Turistica de Paracas* (Tourist Marina). Inside the building, there are kiosks selling tickets for a 2-hour trip to the islands for about $25.00. These boats carry about 20 people and can be difficult for the avid photographer. Check online for other tours in smaller groups or even a private tour for you and yours.

The Candelabro Geoglyph, on the north cliffs of the Paracas Peninsula, about a half-hour before docking at Puerto San Martín. This, of course, is not a candelabra; archaeologists differ on its meaning but it most closely resembles a cactus.

Introduction

For decades, if not centuries, archaeologists and historians asserted that civilizations arose only in areas where extensive agriculture was possible—areas such as the Tigris and Euphrates, the Nile, the Indus, and the Yangtze rivers. Without the ability to grow crops and feed a growing population, the academics averred, large settlements and civilizations were impossible.

Then, in the early 1960s, Michael Moseley, an anthropologist at the University of Florida, began doing research along Peru's coastal desert. Anthropologists and archaeologists had already established—and uncovered—evidence of large, sophisticated, and organized cultures and civilizations in a region where extensive agriculture was extremely difficult. River valleys crossed the desert, fed by the snows of the Andes, but these were miniscule when compared, for example, to the Nile delta.

As archaeologists uncovered more and more evidence of extensive human habitation, including garbage dumps, Moseley and other scientists made a startling discovery: over 90 percent of the protein people had ingested came from the sea. Moseley named this discovery the MFAC hypothesis—the Maritime Foundation of Andean Civilization.[2] In short, societies fed by fishing, rather than agriculture, could have founded a civilization.

The hypothesis, as Moseley told Charles Mann, was "radical, unwelcome, and critiqued as an economic impossibility"[3]. It was paradigm-breaking, and no scientist enjoys having his or her paradigm shattered. Moseley's research undermined the long-held archaeological assumption that,

---

[2] This hypothesis has been independently confirmed by other scholars; for example, Karen Harvey Coutts, Alejandr|o Chu and John Krigbaum, "Paleodiet in Late Preceramic Peru: Preliminary Isotopic Data from Bandurria." May 2011. *The Journal of Island and Coastal Archaeology* 6(2):196-210.
[3] Charles Mann. *1491*, p. 208.

fundamentally, all human societies everywhere are alike, no matter how different they might appear.

But, the earliest civilization in coastal Peru *was* fundamentally different from Mesopotamia, Egypt, India, and China: farming was *not* the cornerstone. The supporting evidence was bone analyses, which showed that late Pleistocene coastal people (around 10,700 BCE[4]) got 90 percent of their protein from the sea.[5] Indeed, Vichama, located near the coast southwest of Caral, is called the *"agropesquera"*—fishing industry—civilization.

This pattern continued for thousands of years. Piles of fish bones and mollusks were found at Bandurria and elsewhere, but little evidence of food crops existed. As the centuries passed and people began farming along the river valleys, the evidence suggests that a symbiotic relationship developed between the fishermen and the farmers; archaeological digs inland reveal a mix of seafood and agricultural products, including beans, corn, squash, and cotton.

By the time the Caral-Supe civilization developed in the Rio Supe valley, 184 km (110 mi) north of Lima and 17 km (10.5 mi) inland, its outlying villages spread to the coast, so a mix of seafood and crops is not surprising. Indeed, recent research has confirmed that maize was a dietary staple by 3000 BCE.[6] Still, the sea's bounty continued to provide a significant part of most coastal people's diets beyond the European conquest.

As coastal civilizations developed, from the equator south, each one built on the developments and contributions of their

----

[4] Since the 19th century, science and then other fields adopted the politically neutral dating designations of BCE and CE, in place of BC and AD. They are increasingly used in academic publications in many fields. BCE stands for "Before the Common Era", CE for "Common Era".

[5] Wilford, J. N., In Peru, Evidence of an Early Human Maritime Culture. *New York Times*. Sept. 22, 1998. http://www.unl.edu/rhames/monte_verde /peru_clovis.htm

[6] Jonathan Haas, et al., "Evidence for Maize (Zea mays) in the Late Archaic (3000-1800 B,C,) in the Norte Chico Region of Peru." 26 March 2013. Proceedings of the National Academy of Sciences. 110 (13): 4945–4949. doi:10.1073/pnas.1219425110

predecessors, then refined them. There are 50 rivers running from the Andes to the coast, but only three carry water year-round. This meant not only that extensive irrigation systems were required to support growing populations but that the systems had to originate in the mountains and that several had to be connected via canals to ensure a sufficient flow of water during the growing season. In northern and central Peru these canals were above ground. The Nasca, however, took advantage of underground canals and then enhanced them with strategically placed spirals dug into the ground (*cantallocs*) that funneled air down to the water and kept it moving. Regardless of design, these irrigation canals, which allowed farming to develop in the river valleys, along with ceramics, textiles, metallurgy, tools, architecture, and roads, reveal the extraordinary talents and achievements of these people, which continue to be uncovered.

The societies developed hierarchical governance along with increasingly complex cosmologies and religious practices. Many worshiped the sea and the sun; two—the Moche and the Chimú—worshiped the moon. While the Nasca worshiped the sun and the moon, their most important deity was the wind god. Most rulers were men; however, in the Moche Empire, several were women, most notably *La Señora de Cao*, discovered at El Brujo in 2005.[7]

The sophisticated cultures of pre-Columbian Peru forcefully remind us that no one country or region of the world has a monopoly on "civilization."

---

[7] Sutherland, S. Unearthed Peruvian Tomb Confirms That Women Ruled Over Brutal Ancient Culture. 26 Aug 2013. https://www.yahoo.com/news/blogs/ geekquinox/unearthed-peruvian-tomb-confirms-women-ruled-over-brutal-160013738.html

NOTES

Timeline

Peru's pre-history spans at least 15,000 years, with confirmed dating back to 13,000 BCE. The earliest evidence of human habitation, to date, has been found in the Andes, near Ancash (between Lima and Trujillo) and Ayacucho (southeast of Lima half way to Cusco), where hunter-gatherers left their detritus. Evidence of high-altitude settlement has been found at several places in the Andes. A team led by archaeologist Kurt Rademaker was looking for obsidian, which had been found in early coastal villages and was dated to between 10,400 and 9,800 BCE. The obsidian, however, came from Alca, in the department of Arequipa, which suggests base camps or outposts in the Andes contemporary with coastal settlements.[8] Indeed, archaeological digs along the coast have confirmed settlement as early as 10,000 BCE.[9] In other regions, notably inside the caves of Pachacamac, Telarmachay, Junín, and Lauricocha, hunting tools dating back more than 11,000 years have been found.

In 2005, in the Zaña Valley southeast of Chiclayo (three hours north of Trujillo), three 5,400-year-old irrigation canals were discovered. There is also evidence of a possible fourth canal, 6,700 years old. Together these suggest community activity to support improved agriculture at a much earlier date than previously believed—and at least 400 years before Caral.

Fast-forward 2,500 years and we encounter the Chavin, who Peruvian archaeologist Julio C. Tello calls "the mother of all the cultures that later bloomed in the old Peru."[11] From this point cultures rose, fell, and built on their predecessors—until the Incas. The timeline on the next page locates the civilizations discussed in this book among the major civilizations and cultures of pre-Inca Peru. The time-line is not exhaustive; in the last century at least 80 distinct groups have been identified and dated by archaeologists.

---

[8] Kurt Rademaker, Late Ice-Age Human Settlement of the High-Altitude Peruvian Andes. (2014). *Mitteilungen der Gesellschaft für Urgeschichte,* 23 http://www.geo.uni-tuebingen.de/fileadmin/website/arbeitsbereich/ufg/ urgeschichte_quartaeroekologie/publikationen/GFU/2014/03_Rademaker_201 214.pdf; Nathan Collins, Earliest High-Altitude Settlements Found in Peru. Pacific Standard. (Oct 23, 2014). https://psmag.com/earliest-high-altitude-settlements-found-in-peru-874b5859a280

[9] John Nobel Wilford, Peruvian Coastal Site yields pre-Clovis artifacts. *New York Times,* 22 Sept 1998. http://www.unl.edu/rhames/monte_verde/peru_ clovis.htm

[10] Nicholas Bakalar, Ancient Canals in Andes Reveal Early Agriculture. *National Geographic News.* 5 Dec 2005. https://newsnationalgeographic.com/news /2005/12/1205_peru_canals.html.

[11] Quoted in Land of the Inkas, Ancash, Huaraz, and Cordillera Blanca. http://landoftheinkas.com/tours/ancash-huaraz/

NOTES

Timeline: 4000 BCE – 1533 CE

4000 BCE   BANDURRIA   2000 BCE

3500-3200 BCE   CARAL-SUPE   1800 BCE

1800 BCE   VICHAMA   1450 BCE

800 BCE   CHAVIN DE HUANTAR   200 CE

750 BCE   PARACAS   100 CE

1100 BCE   NASCA   650 CE

100 CE   LIMA CULTURE   1532 CE

100 CE   MOCHE   800 CE

900 CE   CHIMÚ   1470 CE

900 CE   ISCHMA   1450 CE

1200 CE   CHANCAY   1450 CE

1200 CE   INCAS   1533 CE

NOTES

Section 1: Pre-Ceramic Civilizations

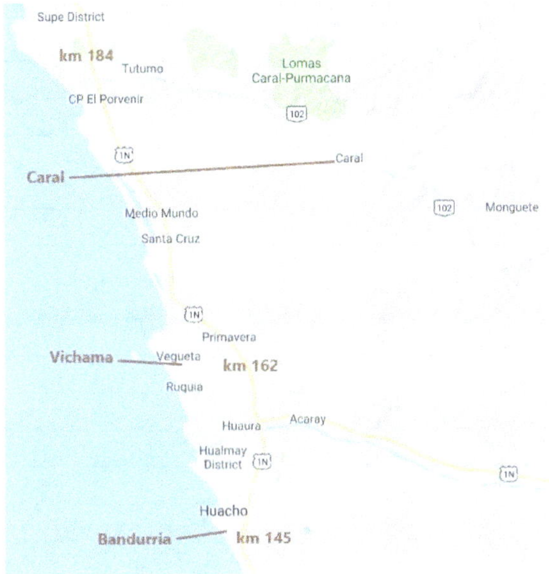

Overview

Until the second decade of the 21st century, it was widely assumed and advertised that Caral, located in the Rio Supe Valley three hours north of Lima, was—at 5,000 years--the oldest urban civilization in the Americas. Carbon dating at Bandurria, 40 km (24 mi) southwest of Caral, upended this claim and placed this coastal site 1,000 years earlier than Caral. Then, as Caral was collapsing, around 1800 BCE, Vichama developed, also along the coast, about halfway between Caral and Bandurria. While there are strong similarities in the architecture among these sites, Vichama reveals a more sophisticated design and advances in artistic development.

In recent years, other coastal sites in Peru have been dated even earlier as the result of recent excavations. They include Sechin Bajo, 330 km (210 mi) northwest of Lima with the oldest radiocarbon dates of 3600 BCE, and Huaricanga, dated to about 3500 BCE, 363 km (236 mi) north of Lima and 59 km (36 mi) north of Caral.

NOTES

1. Bandurria

In the second decade of the twenty-first century, a great debate emerged among Andean archaeologists over how to classify these early civilizations. There is agreement that Bandurria, Caral, and Vichama (along with Aspero—Caral's fishing centre), and other sites form one civilization but…what to call it? "Norte Chico" is used by many; others refer to it as the "pre-ceramic" civilizations because ceramics appear only with the Chavin, around 800 BCE.

All of these early civilizations were pacific; there is no evidence of warfare at any of the sites. Religion was a means of enforcing submission and there is evidence of limited human sacrifice. Bandurria, named for the bird once common in the area, was first excavated by Peruvian archaeologist Rosa Fung in the 1970s and she identified it as a fishing village. In subsequent excavations, Carlos Williams offered a second description: a village with a temple. Then, in 2005, Alejandro Chu arrived to investigate the domestic sector—a "bottom-up" approach--for his doctoral research at the University of Pittsburgh; he is now director of the Bandurria Archaeological Project.

Chu noticed that the dunes in the area weren't "normal"; they were pyramidal. His work led to the discovery of two sectors—the centre with large, ceremonial structures and the periphery with two types of residences: small oval huts made of perishable materials, which historically appeared first, and quadrangular stone buildings with a small ceremonial platform, so identified by items such as unbaked clay figurines. He also found that construction techniques differed from Caral (discussed in #No.2, below); Unlike Caral, Bandurria did not use bamboo for "rebar" but it did use an early form of "gabion wall" (shicra)—rocks and fill in cotton net bags.

Radiocarbon dating of middens of domestic refuse confirms that Bandurria was thriving by 2580 BCE; however, the more rudimentary building materials suggest that it was founded much earlier, thus pre-dating Caral. Indeed, Chu places Bandurria's origins, based on other radiocarbon datings, at 3200 BCE. From its height, Bandurria lasted for over 1,000 years, until 2490 BCE. Its end, like other sites in this guide, may have been caused by a mega-El Niño, which caused the sea life, the primary source of protein, to decline severely. Indeed, Chu's analysis of the contents of the middens from both types of habitations provides further support for the MFAC hypothesis; they reflect, he writes, "a diet based on net-fished species such as anchovy and sardine." (p. 289)

How to Get There

Driving north on the Pan-American highway from Lima, Bandurria is reached by turning left at km 140 and driving 1.1 km. (1/2 mi) to the site, which is on the left. There is a large sign on the highway announcing its location.

The site is 7.4 km (4.5 mi) south of Huacho, the nearest city, from which it is best to take a taxi and have the driver wait.

Visitor Information

Despite its importance as a pre-Caral site and the extensive excavation that has been carried out, Bandurria has not, to date, enjoyed the attention or official promotion that Caral receives. As a result, there is only a small shed where you pay the entrance fee and normally there will be at least two guides on duty. Despite having the same training (a university degree in archaeology/tourism) as guides at other, more well-known sites, in 2018, the guides at Bandurria relied on visitors for their income. More recent information was unavailable at the time of publication.

Because of this, a generous tip is suggested at the end. The guide's English may be limited but they make up for it in knowledge and enthusiasm.

There are porta-potties.

You will be asked to sign a visitor's register and pay a S/7.00 entrance fee (cash only).

Access: Bandurria is completely flat and the route, from which you cannot stray, is a big square that takes you south to the ceremonial pyramids, then west to the cliff that looks down on wetlands, north toward Huacho, paralleling an old railroad track, then northeast back to the entrance.

Exploring the Site

Only the ceremonial area of Bandurria is open to the public; the domestic area, excavated by Chu, lies south of the pyramids and out of sight. There are six plazas, two of which are excavated, and 10 unexcavated pyramids. Leaving the entrance, you will walk south 200m (650 ft) to the first observation area, where you will have a panoramic view of the main pyramid, a broad plaza, and another, later temple on the right. In front of the Centre and Late Temples are sunken plazas, the one on the right significantly larger than the other.

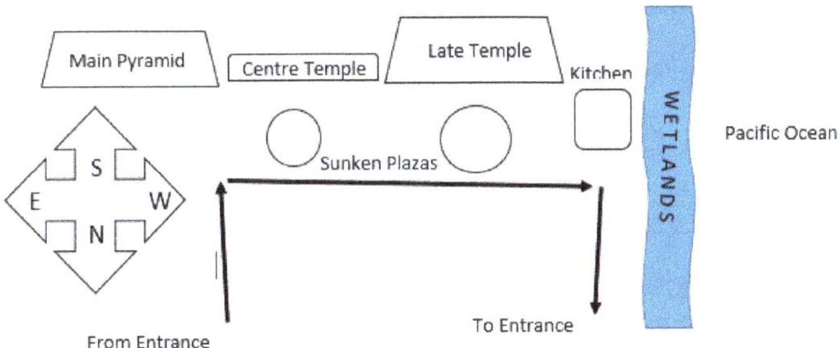

The larger, sunken plaza in front of the Late Temple (above) is completely reconstructed and has dramatic acoustic qualities.

Between the Late Temple and the cliff that drops down to the Albufera El Paraiso Wetlands, is an excavated area that has been identified as a large kitchen (below). The middens found in this area included large quantities of seafood and a number of burnt rocks.

The wetlands, which extend for 7 km (4.2 mi), are home to 125 species of birds, many of them migratory; 33 plants, five species of fish, and five reptiles. Evidence clearly indicates that these wetlands existed in Bandurria's time but a 1945 aerial map shows no wetlands at all. In 1973, however, there was major rainfall in the area, a result of El Niño, which shook loose the earth and opened up the aquifer that fed the wetlands. Within years, flora and fauna had returned and today thrive.

2. Caral

Website: http://www.zonacaral.gob.pe (in Spanish)

Located in the Rio Supe valley, where farming continues to this day, the civilization known as *Caral-Supe* (AKA *Norte Chico*) first settled about 9210 BCE. It would take another 6,000 years for it to become the earliest, confirmed urban centre in the Americas, contemporaneous with the Egyptian pyramids: 5,000-4,000 BCE. Its age has been confirmed by 42 radiocarbon datings. At its peak *Caral-Supe* included about 30 population centres stretching north, south, and west to the coast. The city of Caral, at its peak, extended over 626 hectares (2.4 mi²), had 32 public buildings, several residential areas, and a population of about 3,000. In the valley, however, there are 19 other sites, so the total population of the area may have been as high as 20,000.

During my first visit in 2010, our guide Roosevelt (no kidding!), told us that all the local people knew of the mounds but no one had ever asked *them*[8]—until the mounds were "discovered" in 1994 via aerial photography. Excavations began after Peruvian archaeologist Ruth Shady Solis visited the area and confirmed that the "hills" were really pyramids covered with several millennia of sand. After 10 years of serious excavation and restoration, the site opened to the public in 2006 and was named a UNESCO World Heritage Site in 2009.

Roosevelt was well-spoken and well informed. He is from the area and, for seven years, worked on excavation. When he was offered the opportunity to train as a guide at Caral, he seized it and began leading tours in 2006. All of the workers and guides at the site are locals; only the archaeologists come from Lima.

The ensuing years of excavation, restoration, and conservation have revealed six pyramids, two temples, a large

---

[8] This recalls the search for the lost Franklin Expedition in northern Canada. The Inuit knew where the *Erebus* and *Terror* were, but no one listened to them until Parks Canada assumed responsibility for the search and included Inuit on the team. The *Erebus* was discovered, intact, in 2014, the *Terror* in 2016—the latter exactly where Inuit said it was.

amphitheatre, and living quarters. Between 2010 and 2013, a much larger area of Caral was opened, increasing the area available to visitors by at least 25 percent.

There are low mountains on three sides, which meant that access was controlled and easy only from the west. There was a sophisticated government and monumental architecture but almost no ceramics or art. Caral was a non-militarized society and essentially a theocracy. Religion dominated life and was used by the ruling class to ensure social cohesion and cultural identity—as well as exercise control.

Caral made two lasting contributions to later civilizations. On the religious side, a gourd found at the site in 2002 bears the image of a god, which has come to be known as the Staff God. The figure is sharp-toothed, wears a hat, and has a long stick or rod in each hand. Archaeologists debate its significance and whether it is merely a convention—comparable, say, to distant future archaeologists uncovering crucifixes and trying to determine whether they refer to one man or many. It is clear that the Staff God was the beginning of a spiritual tradition that endured for millennia and, over 4,000 years, evolved into Wiraqocha, the Inca creator god.

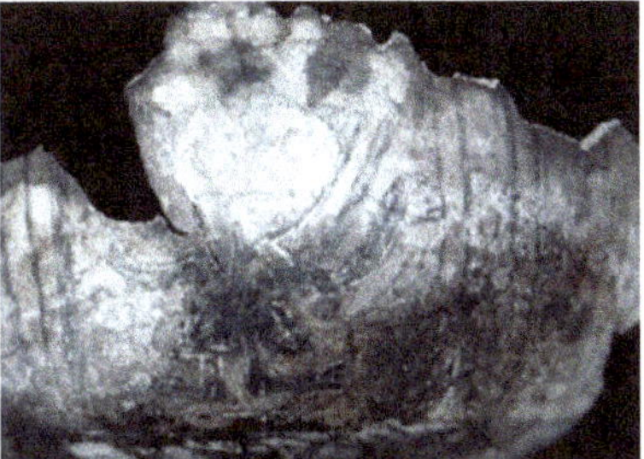

Caral Gourd-Photo: Jonathon Haas; Depiction in C. Mann, 1491, p. 211;

Staff God on Urn, Larco Museum; Wiraqocha statue, Sacred Valley

The second contribution was the *quipu*. Until the discovery of a rudimentary *quipu* made of llama and alpaca hair in the Gallery Pyramid, there was a general assumption that *quipus* developed much later. But, the earliest *quipu* (so far)—the string-and-knot method of keeping records that the Incas elevated to a high art—comes from Caral.

Quipu found at Caral.

Caral apparently engaged in limited human sacrifice, but its purpose is unknown. In the largest of the six pyramids, the body of a teenager was found, his fingers missing, three blows to the skull, hands tied behind his back, and naked. However, a cemetery with four children carefully buried, each wrapped in a shroud with semi-precious stones inside, has been found. Conclusion: these children were loved and their loss was mourned.

It is not known where the *Caral-Supe* came from. They could have come down from the mountains or from the earlier civilizations that have recently been identified 60 km (36 mi) and 190 km (113 mi) to the north. They might have migrated from across the sea; or they may have been a continuation of the migration from Asia across the land mass that covered what is now the Bering Strait.

We do know that they had a sophisticated knowledge of mathematics, geometry, architecture, music, and astronomy. Excavations have uncovered 37 cornets made of deer and llama bones and 33 flutes, the latter radiocarbon dated to between 2190 and 2170 BCE, along with about 100 unfired clay human figurines, many of them women. They dug irrigation canals, engaged in agricultural experimentation, and produced enough food to feed all their people.

In 2016, a 4,500-year-old tomb holding the mummy of a high-ranking woman was discovered at Aspero, a "suburb" of Caral 25 km (15 mi) WNW near the coast. It confirms that Caral was a gender-equal society in which women held political, religious, and leadership roles—almost five millennia before La Señora de Cao (see No. 3) ruled at El Brujo.[9]

Caral challenges the hypothesis that warfare was *the* reason for organizing into cities. This sacred, peaceful city, which lasted a millennium, demonstrates that, like the MFAC hypothesis, there is never a unicausal explanation for any social phenomenon.

Caral would lay abandoned for many centuries until later cultures occupied the city. The Chavin (900-200 BCE) would add their identifiable architectural touches, most notably protrusions on the gallery Pyramid—seen in the centre-right oval in the image on the next page.

---

[9] Shivali Best and Janet Tappin Coelho. "Face of the Lady with the Four Brooches, a Peruvian noble in the gender/equal Caral civilisation, is revealed with a reconstruction of her 4,500-year-old skull." 11 October 2017. http://www.dailymail.co.uk/sciencetech/article-4969214/Scientists-recreate-face-4-500-year-old-Peruvian-mummy.html

It is also not known what happened to them. Caral thrived for 1,000 years, and then disappeared. There is no evidence of invasion or warfare. There are two theories, Roosevelt said: The first is that severe climate change, perhaps caused by El Niño, brought drought and starvation, forcing abandonment of the city; the second is that the influence of new civilizations, further to the north, caused them to abandon Caral and move elsewhere. Regardless of cause, evidence suggests that a significant number of people from Caral moved southeast to Vichama, which was founded after Caral collapsed.

Then, 1,400 years later the Chancay civilization, which arose north of Lima, would leave its mark with buildings between the original Caral footprint and the Rio Supe. The Chancay were significantly more advanced with a ceremonial system and complex cosmology that was reflected in their mortuary practices. They also had sophisticated ceramics and textiles.

Chancay buildings in foreground.

Further research may reveal what happened to the *Caral-Supe* people; meanwhile, Caral reminds us that human beings can do extraordinary things with minimal tools and resources, and that the Western Hemisphere has a human history and cultures as rich and fascinating as anywhere else in the world.

How to Get There

Caral is a three-hour drive north of Lima. Take the Pan-American Highway north to km 184. The turn-off to Caral is well-marked. Head east for another 25 km, away from the coast and up a narrow, paved road. I say "up" because the road climbs gently all the way and, on arrival you are close to the Andean foothills at an elevation of 350 m (1,148 ft) above sea level. Signs will direct you to the parking areas. From there a 20 to 30-minute walk will take you across the Rio Supe to the entrance; however, there is parking closer to the entrance for tour buses and people with mobility issues.

Pre-arranged tours from Lima range upward from $196.00 per person and take about 12 hours; however, you can rent a car or hire a taxi at your hotel to take you. Negotiate the price before leaving and plan on at least S/50.00 per hour—for two to three people. Remember that gas/petrol is expensive and there are tolls. Getting out of Lima, follow signs to the airport (*aeropuerto*). This puts you on the Pan-American Highway and, once past the airport, driving is easy. Some of the Pan-Am is four lanes; all of it is fairly new, wide, and well-maintained.

Tip: Depart early from Lima, for two reasons. The traffic becomes progressively worse as the day wears on so leaving by 07:00 is optimal. And, because it can get very hot, arriving early at Caral means you will begin your tour in the coolest part of the day.

Visitor Information

Caral is open daily from 09:00 to 17:00, but the last entrance is at 15:00. This is because it takes at least two hours to walk the site.

Cost: Adults: S/11.00; Seniors (60+) at all archaeological sites are half-price; Students and Teachers: S/4.00; Children: S/1.00

There is shade, a snack bar, washrooms, and a lovely small museum at the entrance. There is no shade walking around the site, so bring a hat, comfortable walking shoes, sunscreen, and a water bottle.

You must be part of a private tour or use one of the tour guides at the entrance. The guides, some of whom speak English, are all well-trained and licenced. Many of them have participated in the excavations at Caral. There is no charge for their services; a tip at the end is appropriate and welcome.

Access: Caral is flat so it is easy to move around the site. There are a few steps at certain pyramids that may or may not be open to visitors.

Exploring the Site

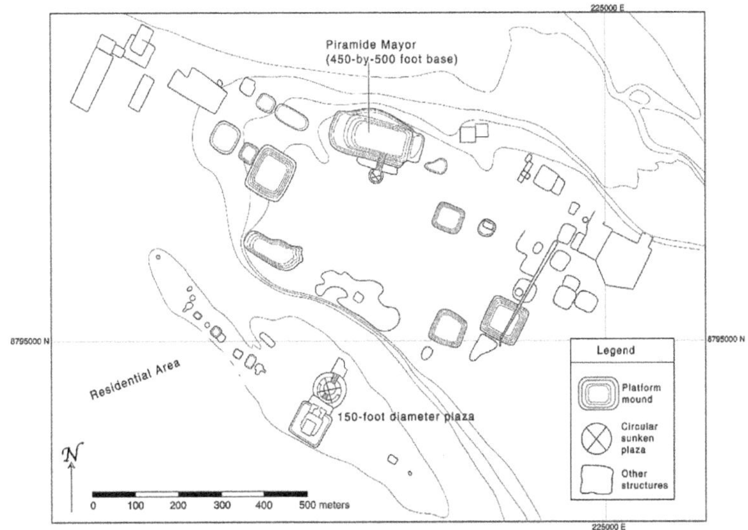

Map Courtesy of Field Museum. http://www.freerepublic.com/focus/f-news/1724450/posts

Caral covers a wide area, more than 626 hectares (1,547 acres). Plan at least 90 minutes to walk the entire circuit; two hours is better, especially for photographers. The walkways are clearly defined with small rocks on each side. You may be fortunate enough to see archaeologists at work and, if you speak Spanish, to chat briefly with them.

Layout. It is likely that Caral was envisioned as a calendar and each public building was connected to a deity and astral location. Various activities occurred in each building on holidays. The city is divided into Upper and Lower Caral. Upper Caral includes pyramids and residential complexes around the Great Central Plaza. Lower Caral, to the south, had one large avenue and the Amphitheatre is the primary feature. In the southeastern area, an astronomical laboratory has been uncovered.

Building materials. The people of Caral had no ceramics and no metal implements. They used two types of stone for construction: granite from the mountains and river rocks from the Rio Supe. The blue river rocks, being harder than the granite, were used to chip away the granite blocks that were used in construction. Minimal polishing was done to the rocks that were used for pyramid, temple, or residential facades.

Building Materials: Granite and River Rocks.

There are six pyramids of varying sizes, each with three sets of stairs. These reveal that, like the Maya of southern Mexico and northern Central America, they built a larger pyramid on top of the existing one, all with flat tops—just like many lowland Mayan pyramids centuries later.

The Central Esplanade, below, an enormous plaza, includes several small plazas and buildings. The Great Pyramid is in the distance.

La Huanca pyramid (below) has a vertical stone 2.15 m tall and set 2.3 m into the ground about 10 m (32 ft) from its steps. The stone is associated with astronomical and ceremonial activities. Theories are that it was either a solar clock or a marker from which the location of other pyramids and buildings was determined.

There are residential areas within the site and on the outskirts. Houses for the upper class and priests were a fairly decent size, about 10m long and at least as wide. Each of the houses has a small fire pit near the front entrance and a flue that runs out to the street (below). Archaeologists believe that these fires were kept burning 24/7, perhaps to keep out evil spirits, perhaps to warm the "foyer," perhaps both. The Lesser Plaza is bordered by the Lesser Pyramid and the E2-E3 building.

The Caral-Supe figured out that it was efficient to make nets from plants and vines to carry the rocks from the nearby hills and river—but they also figured out that leaving the rocks in the nets provided a very good way to fill foundations and provide supporting walls. We saw the remains of these nets and rocks in one building being excavated. The modern incarnation of these nets are metal—often chicken wire—and we call them "gabion walls". The builders of Caral also used bamboo as an early form of rebar, which was exposed near the bags of rocks.

Nets with rocks and bamboo.

The Great Plaza's main attraction is the Great Pyramid, which was a major ceremonial and administrative centre. From its top, rulers could monitor both activities in the city and in a good part of the valley.

On the north side of the site are two temples, one connected to a large amphitheatre. Archaeologists think the amphitheatre was used for communal celebrations that people of all classes attended. Afterward, however, the priests would go into the temple just north of the arena for their religious rituals, which no one else could attend. The rectangular flat stone on the left side has a petroglyph etched on top: a monkey. Because monkeys live only in the jungle—more than 200 km (120 mi) east on the other side of the Andes—this petroglyph (flat stone on centre left in the following picture) offers compelling evidence of early intercultural exchange between Amazonia and the coast.

NOTES

3. Vichama

Website: http://www.zonacaral.gob.pe/en/news-2/city-vichama
-an-ancient-narrative/

Discovered in 2007, Vichama was initially thought to be a peripheral settlement of Caral. However, excavations revealed that Vichama emerged around 1800 B.C., after the collapse of Caral, possibly settled by migrants from Caral who took architecture and design to new levels. Vichama lasted at least 300 years, then centuries later would be occupied by the Chancay, followed by Chimú.

Vichama began in the midst of drought and food shortages; there was a severe climate change between 1850 and 1800 BCE. These conditions produced some of the most dramatic reliefs of pre-Columbian Peru, which are described below.

The site sits on a significant elevation in the landscape that protected it from the torrential rains and floods produced by El Niño. It extends over 136 ha. (336 acres) and includes 22 buildings, nine of which have had substantial excavation; however, archaeological work continues at all of them. Construction methods were similar to those of Caral and were earthquake-resistant.

Vichama is located on the south side of the road opposite the fishing/agricultural village of Végueta and calls itself the "*agropesquera* (fishing industry) civilization", 800m (2,500 ft) from the sea.

How to get there

In March 2018 there was no large sign on the road announcing the location of Vichama (unlike Bandurria and Caral). The turnoff is at km 159 on the Pan-American Highway and you have to look for it. You may see a sign for Végueta, but we missed it and turned off at km 161, then backtracked along a parallel road, the old Pan-American Highway, to a junction where there is a small sign for Vichama and a larger sign for Végueta. From this junction it is just over 4 km (2.4 mi) to Vichama, on the left. From the Pan-Am it is just over 5 km.

Visitor information

Vichama is open from 09:00 to 17:00. There is a small building that serves as a welcome center and where entrance tickets (S/11, half-price for seniors over 60) can be purchased. Like most of the other sites discussed in this guide, you must have a guide to tour Vichama and they are very knowledgeable, as many of them have worked at the excavation. All signage is bilingual (Spanish and English).

Access. Unlike Bandurria and Caral, Vichama is a bit hilly but the slopes are gentle. It is necessary to climb a 30° ramp to reach the interior of *Las Hornacinas*, where the relief figures are located. After walking through the building, the exit is down some stairs. These are the only steps on the site, at least in the structures open during our visit. The paths are smooth dirt, so there should be no problem with a walker.

Exploring the site

Beyond the entrance, the first stop will be the beautifully preserved amphitheater, a sunken plaza about 10 m (31 ft) in diameter. Continuing along the path you will reach the buildings of Sector A, *Las Hornacinas* (top left on the map), which has two facades and three levels, the latter built at different times. The original entrance faces north, towards Caral and Aspero, where these people came from. After entering through the ramp, the three levels are exposed on the right.

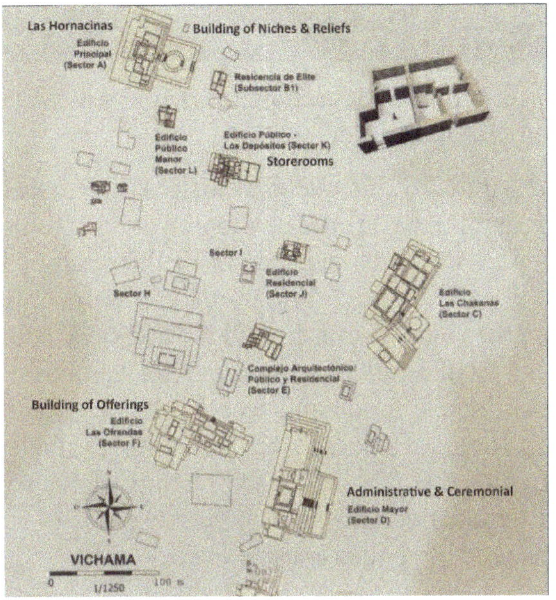

Adapted by the author from the original site plan at Vichama.

At the top, in the back, there is a toad peeking out from the bottom of the wall with a lightning bolt above its head. The toads are not endemic to coastal Peru; they come from the forest many miles inland, and as our guide, Xander Astete, pointed out, "when the toad starts croaking, it's going to rain." The toad, then, is a symbol of rain, the basic necessity for crops and life.

In front of the frog are two levels with dramatic reliefs that help tell the story of Vichama. The lower level has a row of humans in great distress: emaciated, anguish in their faces, an upside-down couple. These figures are clearly a reference to the great famine and suffering caused by extreme drought over a period of years. The upper lever, however, shows healthy figures, engaged in ritual activities, possibly dancing.

Further on are two fish reliefs, clearly a tribute to the main source of protein in the diet.

After leaving *Las Hornacinas*, a right turn takes you up a gently sloping hill past an elite residential center (Subsector B1), the only one of the three subsectors in this area to have been excavated so far. A little further on are some minor public buildings on the right (Sector L) and a warehouse complex (The Warehouses) on the left (Sector K). The warehouses enjoyed three stages of construction and reconstruction, expanding each time. Here, some of the most interesting artifacts found at Vichama include the unbaked head of a high-status woman; two heads from female human statues; a basket made of reeds; and a fishhook made from a giant mussel shell.

After passing through a residential sector (J) and continuing uphill, the next stop is the Sector, an area that began as a small ceremonial center then expanded during a second period, but was eventually partially demolished, buried, and replaced by a residential group.

Near the top of the hill is *Las Ofrendas*, the Offerings Building (Sector F), which includes a central stairway, platforms, a ceremonial hall, and other rooms. Originally, there were two buildings, but over time they were remodeled and joined to create one large building with a stepped design. Among the offerings found here was a group of seven gourds that had been placed at the base of the building's façade.

Near the top of *Cerro Halconcillo*, on the east side, is Vichama's largest building: the Great Building (Sector D), which was one of the governmental centers. This is the first building with a square floor plan and a 5m (16 ft) wide staircase leading to the ceremonial hall. Later they extended the building to the south, building new platforms and a second ceremonial hall. They have discovered part of a relief, a hand holding an instrument. It is not surprising, then, that flutes made of bone, including the bone of a camelid (llama or alpaca), were found in the building. As camelids are endemic to the Andes, an instrument made of camelid bone suggests some level of exchange between the coast and the mountains as early as 1800 BC.

The summit of Halconcillo Hill offers a 360-degree view of the Huaura Valley and the Pacific Ocean. As you descend, you reach the last major complex: *Las Chakanas* (Sector C). The *Chakana*, or Andean Cross, appears in architecture and art throughout the region, from Tiahuanaco on Lake Titicaca to a tattoo on a mummy in the Maria Reiche Museum in the province of Nasca. At Vichama, the *Chakanas* centre includes three monumental architectural components, each with its own stairway, ceremonial hall and auxiliary rooms. The façade of the southernmost unit was decorated with niches forming the *Chakana*. In the central section, a long stone was found with figures painted in red. There are paintings of the sun and moon and, on top of the structure are stones representing each celestial object. This tells us that these people had astronomical knowledge that told them when to plant and when to fish.

Excavations continue at Vichama and, in 2018, a 1m by 2.8m (3.2 by 9.2 ft) wall carving was uncovered at the entrance of a ceremonial hall. The relief depicts four human heads with their eyes closed and two snakes passing around them. The serpents' heads point to a humanized seed that is digging into the soil. According to Ruth Shady Solis, who supervises the site, the serpents represent a water god that irrigates the earth and makes seeds grow.

https://www.elcomercio.com/tendencias/descubrimiento-mural-peru-vichama-arqueologia.html

Section 2: The Moche

History

There is a consensus that the Moche civilization emerged from the remnants of the Chavin culture, which began to develop around 1200 BCE and lasted until about 300 BCE, when social upheaval caused the abandonment of the main sites. Moving forward 400 years, the Moche culture began to take shape along the northern coast of Peru. Eventually, it extended 402 km (241 mi) along the coast and 80 km (48 mi) inland. Its influence would extend as far as the Chincha Islands, 13 km (8 mi) west of Pisco.

Several autonomous regions emerged, the two most important being Moche Sur in the Huacas de Moche, near Trujillo, and Moche Norte in Sipán, near Chiclayo. Three general periods have been identified: Early Intermediate (100-550 CE), Middle Horizon (550-950 CE), and Late Intermediate

(950-1200 CE), with the peak of the Moche civilization between 100 and 800 CE. The sites included here are all Southern Moche.

Governance. Although the Moche were not a monolithic polity, some regard it as the first state in South America. Other archaeologists, however, argue that, absent stronger evidence to support the "first state" theory, it is possible that several incipient states developed along the northern Peruvian coast in the centuries before the rise of the Moche.[10] Two distinct but related languages were spoken, Muchic in the north and Quingan in the south. The various autonomous states--similar to Mayan city-states--shared a hierarchical social structure and cultural values.

In the end, some evidence suggests, climate change marked the beginning of the end. Between 536 and 594 CE, it is possible that a super El Niño caused 30 years of heavy rains and floods, followed by 30 years of drought. These extremes may have led to the breakdown of the Moche's faith in their gods and the efficacy of human sacrifice, which contributed to social unrest and political disintegration. Other evidence, however, indicates that Moche states continued beyond 650 CE, notably in the Moche valley south of Trujillo.

Agriculture. Unlike the earliest coastal societies, the Moche world was based on agriculture, which was maintained by a large system of irrigation canals. Maize (corn), beans, squash, cotton, and other crops were supplemented by rich harvests from the sea. In the Moche Valley alone, it is estimated that agriculture supported a population of about 25,000.

Religion. There were two main gods in the Moche pantheon. *Aí Apaec*, the creator or sun god, was believed to dwell in the high Andes. In Moche art he usually has large fangs, snake earrings, and a jaguar headdress- -similar to the Staff God.

---

[10] Jean-François Millaire. Formation of primary states in the Virú valley, northern coast of Peru. Proceedings of the National Academy of Sciences. (2010, March 22), pp. 6186-6191. doi: 10.1073/pnas.0911226107

Si, the moon goddess, was considered the supreme deity because she controlled the weather, which affected both agriculture and daily life. Like the Chimú who followed, for the Moche the moon was considered more powerful than the sun because *Si* was visible day and night.

A third god, often depicted in Moche art, is the Decapitator, so called because he is usually depicted with a *tumi* (crescent-shaped ceremonial knife) in one hand and a severed head in the other.[11] The photo below left depicts a Moche decapitation.

Human sacrifice was an important aspect of Moche beliefs; both Moche prisoners of war and citizens were offered to appease *Aí Apaec*, with their blood offered in ceremonial cups. At Huaca de la Luna, the remains of 40 men, all under the age of 30, reveal that they were mutilated before being thrown from the top of the pyramid; their bones have gashes; arms and legs were ripped out of sockets, and they were beheaded. Given that the skeletons were found on the surface, softened by heavy El Niño rains, it is possible that the sacrifices were intended to appease the Moche gods and ward off environmental disaster.

---

[11] The decapitator also appears in the Pukara civilization, which arose in the high Andes about an hour northwest of Puno and Lake Titicaca, 200 BCE-400 CE. Photo top right.

Culture. The Moche were contemporaries of the Nasca and Moche pottery has been found near Ica, north of Nasca, although no Nasca pottery has been found in the Moche region. Moche contributions to pre-Columbian art are numerous; they include architecture, brilliant jewelry design, painted ceramics, textiles, and extensive friezes.

Architecture. Around 450 CE, the Moche began building their most important ceremonial center, anchored by two massive pyramids. The *Huaca del Sol* is (to date) the largest pre-Columbian structure in Peru and was built with more than 140 million adobe bricks, each bearing the mark of its maker. The four levels of the pyramid were originally 50 m (164 ft) high and had a surface area of 340 m (1,115 ft) by 160 m (525 ft) (54,400 m^2--177,000 ft^2)[12]; however, after the conquest, the Spanish heavily damaged it in their quest for gold and silver, which knocked 10m (33 ft) off the top.

Five hundred meters (1,640 ft) to the east is the Huaca de la Luna, which has six levels, four of which have been excavated to date. This pyramid is famous for its friezes, which portray Moche cosmology and rituals. Both pyramids were originally painted red, yellow, black, and white, which would have created a dramatic, if not awe-inspiring, contrast with the surrounding sand-coloured desert.

Smaller pyramids have been identified and some have been excavated at other Moche sites, notably at El Brujo, 75 km (46 mi) north of the *huacas*.

Jewelry. The Moche worked with gold, silver, and copper, with stones such as turquoise and shells, in particular the *Spondylus*, which comes from Ecuador and was traded south into the Andes and as far north as Mexico. The Moche regarded the sea and animals as sacred, used *Spondylus* shells in their jewelry and depicted *Spondylus* in their art (photo below).

---

[12] By comparison, the Pyramid of the Sun in Teotihuacan, Mexico, is 220 m by 230 m or 50,600 m^2 and 65 m high.

Creative and skilled artisans created ornate gold headdresses and chest plates, ear-spools, and nose ornaments.

Ceramics. Of all the cultural expressions found in Moche society, their ceramics stand out, not only for their craftsmanship but also for their variety and because they tell us so much about Moche life, from the sublime to the humorous and erotic. Scenes of flora and fauna, hunting, fishing, runners carrying messages, sacrifice, fighting, elaborate ceremonies, and sexual acts reveal details about daily activities that would otherwise have been lost in the absence of a written language. Most famous, however, are the Moche portrait ceramics, which are individualized and tell us that these were real people, not an artist's stylized conception. Indeed, Rick Vecchio, a Lima-based travel agent and guide, theorizes that the Larco Museum may possess a ceramic portrait of the Lord of Sipan![13].

---

[13] Rick Vecchio, "Pre-Columbian ruler's face revealed, but is it his first true portrait?". July 21, 2017. http://www.fertur-travel.com/blog/2017/ face-of-pre-columbian-ruler-revealed-but-is-it-his-first-true-portrait/13043/

Textiles. Compared to the thousands of intact Moche ceramics that have been found, there are relatively few examples of Moche textiles. The surviving pieces tell us that they used cotton, which would have been grown along the coast, as well as alpaca and vicuña, which reveals that they had a flourishing trade with the Andean peoples where these animals live. The designs include geometric motifs, fauna, and gods.

A Moche Creation Story

Once there were two brothers walking together in the field near their village. They came upon a snake — a tiny serpent. The brothers were astonished to see that the serpent had two heads.

They brought the serpent home to keep as a pet. They fed it and the serpent grew. And grew. And grew, so fast and so large that the people in the village became fearful. They told the brothers, "This serpent is too big and it is very dangerous. Get rid of it." The brothers, with heavy hearts, put the serpent in a sack, and walked with it the five kilometers to the ocean shore, where they left It.

Soon after the boys had gone, the serpent managed to escape from the sack. Infuriated at having been abandoned, the two-headed snake followed the boys back to the village, devouring every animal and person in its path, until it arrived — enormous, spectacularly large — to seek vengeance.

The villagers were unable to defend themselves against the monstrous beast. One group of villagers ran away, toward the White Mountain. The serpent gave chase. They ran up the mountain's slope, the serpent in close pursuit.

Just when they were about to be eaten by the serpent, the mountain opened up. The people entered and the serpent followed, and the mountain snapped shut, a black line on the side of the mountain marks the scar where it opened and shut. The rest of the people who witnessed what happened, to honour the mmountain that saved them—the God of the Mountain—built the Huaca de la Luna.

NOTES

4. Huaca de la Luna

Website: http://www.huacasdemoche.pe

How to Get There

Huaca de la Luna and Huaca del Sol are located on the Rio Moche about 10 km (6 mi) and a 20-minute drive south of Trujillo on the road to the port of Salaverry. From the port, where cruise ships dock, it is also about a 20-minute drive. The turn-off is well-marked, and one drives through the town of Moche en route. Several tour companies offer tours of the Moche capital, leaving from hotels in the area. You can book a tour in advance of arrival through several online Peruvian travel agencies. Alternatively, you can negotiate with a taxi driver to take you to the site and wait for you. As it is isolated—4 km (2.4 mi) from a major road—having a driver is the best policy. The third option is to take a *Combi,* a local bus that passes Ovalo Grau in Trujillo about every 15 minutes.

Visitor Information

The site is open Monday-Friday from 09:00 to 16:30, Saturday and Sunday from 09:00 to 13:00. Admission is S/10, half-price for seniors, to the site. A licenced guide is included with the price of admission and you will be given a tour time with your ticket. Allow about 90 minutes to visit the Huaca de la Luna.

There is a lovely museum, the *Museo Huacas de Moche*, which has opened in the last decade and visiting it, before going through the Huaca de la Luna is highly recommended. Museum admission is S/5 and, while signage is in English and Spanish, a guide will add many interesting details. The museum will take 30-45 minutes and offers information about the history, culture, politics, and religion of the Moche in addition to a wonderful collection of artifacts found during excavations. Washrooms are available in the museum and at the entrance to the Huaca.

Footwear, especially for older folks, is important at Huaca de la Luna, Huaca Rajada, Tucume, El Brujo, and other sites with inclined earthen paths, which can be treacherous if you're wearing flat-soled shoes or sneakers. Cross trainers or hiking boots are recommended.

You may well see a *biringo* or two, the famous Peruvian hairless dog, whose body temperature is higher than other dogs. As a result, they have long been used as body warmers for people with various ailments, including arthritis.

Biringo -- Hairless dog

Access: There is a long ramp up to the entrance of the Huaca because one begins at the top of the pyramid and works one's way down to the lowest excavated level. There are six levels and four have, to date, been excavated. Inside there are stairways connecting the various levels as well as long walkways.

The **Huaca del Sol** (above), which is the largest pre-Columbian edifice in Peru, sits about 500m (1/4 mi) west of the Huaca de la Luna and is undergoing excavation. It is not open to the public. You will pass it on your way to the site entrance.

The discovery of tombs inside the structure suggests that it was a ceremonial site. About one-third of the pyramid has been washed away but it is estimated that 140 million bricks were used in its construction. Many of the bricks have symbols etched into them—marks of the workers who made them. Like the Huaca de la Luna, Sol has several levels with steep stairways, ramps, and walls with a 77-degree slope. Sadly, 1500 years of weather and human damage have left the pyramid looking like a mound of adobe bricks, covered with sand.

The **Huaca de la Luna,** however, is an archaeologist's dream. It is, in fact, two temples, representing the beginning and the end of the Moche civilization. Its rooms contained ceramics, gold, and silver; the *in situ* friezes of stylized figures—many of them perfectly preserved by the layers built on top—spread across several levels.

From the top of the Huaca de la Luna—the first level—the White Mountain towers over it. This was the most important ceremonial area of the Huaca. There are rooms adjacent to the altar where priests dressed for the ceremonies. The altar, a short distance away, reveals extensive signs of burning and 40 decapitated, mutilated bodies were found nearby. Ten skeletons had their hands bound and had been garroted. Archaeologists theorize that soldiers were an honoured caste; therefore, it was an honour to die in the ceremony.

The White Mountain with the ceremonial area in front. The pile of Black stones on the lower left is the altar area

From the priests' rooms, it is a short walk down to the second level, where the iconic symbol of the Huaca de la Luna—the decapitation murals —can be seen.

Continuing down a flight of about 12 steps brings you to the third level, which is dated between 001 CE and 199 CE. Here you will see the most extensive murals and a panel of Moche myths.

The fourth and most recently excavated level lies immediately north of the third level. Here is a large plaza and more murals. From this point you must walk back up the ramp that brought you down to the lowest level, through the ceremonial area, and down the entry ramp.

NOTES

5. El Brujo Huaca Cao Viejo

Website: http://www.elbrujo.pe/en/

History

The first human settlements in this area date back 5,000 years, contemporaneous with Caral. El Brujo, the Moches' most important shrine, was constructed in the first centuries of the Common Era (CE) and was used for about 800 years.

How to Get There

El Brujo (The Witch or Shaman) is located on the Pacific coast in the Chicama Valley, 60 km (36 mi) north of Trujillo on the Pan-American Highway, then 25 km (13 mi) west to the site. The exit from the Pan-Am is well marked and signage along the access road, which takes you through the town of Magdalena de Cao, is excellent.

There are three ways to comfortably visit El Brujo: take a tour from Trujillo, hire a driver; or rent a car in Trujillo and drive yourself. Trying to arrive by bus will take at least half a day because, unlike the Huaca de la Luna, there is no local bus service to the site. There are buses from Trujillo to Chicope (50 min), from where you can hire a taxi to reach El Brujo. Alternatively, you can take a local bus from Chicope to Magdalena de Cao (20 minutes), then a motorcycle taxi to El Brujo (10 min).

Visitor Information

El Brujo is open daily from 09:00 to 16:00 (the last admission is at 15:00). Plan to spend 90 minutes to two hours.

Admission is S/10.00 for adults, S/5.00 for retired Peruvians and university students, and S/1.00 for school children. This fee includes the museum.

There is a wonderful museum with artifacts from the site, including La Señora de Cao and other mummies. Your guide will recommend that you visit the museum *after* visiting the site;

take his or her advice. Although photography is forbidden in the museum, at the end, you will have the opportunity to dress up in Moche attire and have your guide take your picture.

There are trained guides on site, several of whom speak excellent English. There is no charge for the guides but a healthy tip is recommended and well-deserved.

Access: The large courtyard with magnificent friezes are easily accessible as a long, gradual ramp leads you to the site; however, climbing steps is necessary to view the areas that have been excavated up and behind the courtyard, and there are gentle steps down from the mausoleum area where *La Señora de Cao* was buried.

El Brujo complex from the north.

Exploring the Site

El Brujo gets its name from the fact that shamans (or witches) regularly used—and still use—the site for ceremonial purposes. A shaman, who lives in Magdalena de Cao, regularly uses the *Pozo Ceremonial* (ceremonial well, discovered in 2004) for cleansing, re-birthing, and purification ceremonies.

As with all other pre-Columbian buildings along the coast, adobe construction was used through at least seven building phases. Walking up to the ceremonial plaza (the first stop), you will pass a long-abandoned Catholic monastery.

The first stop in the complex is the large ceremonial courtyard, enclosed on three sides with a long platform. Running along the back of the platform is a long frieze of slaves walking.

To the left of the courtyard are steps leading up and behind it.

43

To the left of the courtyard are steps leading up and behind it. Another small courtyard leads to a large room where decapitator murals are visible and one has been restored (above)

On the west side of the courtyard is a single door entry into a large chamber with more friezes and tombs, dating from the eighth century CE in which members of the Moche elite were buried (above).

La Señora de Cao. El Brujo's claim to fame resides in a platform on the north side of the main courtyard and a few steps down from the mausoleum. Here, in 2005, archaeologists discovered the perfectly preserved mummy of a tattooed woman in her mid- to late-20s. She had borne at least one child not long before she died and had an abscessed wisdom tooth; otherwise, her body revealed no pathologies. She died about 450 CE.

Foreground: La Señora de Cao's tomb; teenager's and other tombs behind

Her elaborate burial confirmed that this was a powerful woman in the Moche hierarchy, probably the ruler of the Chicama Valley; indeed, she has been compared to the Lord of Sipán, who lived in the late third century CE and whose untouched tomb was discovered in 1987.14 She was buried with 15 necklaces of lapis lazuli, quartz, silver, and/or a gold-copper alloy around her neck and 100 metal objects around her, including 60 of pure gold. Nearby, three men and one teenage boy, who may have been relatives, were buried. The boy had been sacrificed; he was found in a fetal position in a small tomb just south of La Señora, and his function was probably to serve as a guard in the afterlife. =

---

14 The museum does not yet have a website. For information on the Lord of Sipán see http://www.go2peru.travel/peru_guide/chiclayo/sipan_museum.htm, which includes an article written by Dr. Walter Alva, the Peruvian archaeologist who discovered the tomb, and https://www.world-archaeology.com/features/tombs -of-the-lords-of-sipan.htm

The walls around the tombs (above) are colourfully decorated with figures from Moche iconography that also appear in *La Señora's* tattoos and funerary attire, including spiders, fish, snakes, cats, and celestial figures.

The Larco Museum
The World's Greatest Collection of Moche Art

In the early 1920s young Rafael Larco returned from ten years of schooling in the United States, including a degree in agricultural engineering from Cornell and additional studies in business administration. He planned to help run the family's sugar cane plantation and other business interests near Trujillo. That was before an uncle gave Rafael's father 600 pieces of pre-Columbian pottery and other artifacts.

While Rafael never completely abandoned the family's businesses, the collection refocused his time and energy. Archaeology was in its early days and the engineer developed a rigorous, scientific method for identifying and cataloging the artifacts. In 1926 he opened a museum—named for his beloved father—to display them.

Over the next 15 years Rafael would acquire several more collections, add to them with his own excavations, continue his research, and in so doing become a founder of Peruvian archaeology. Larco focused on the civilizations spread along the Pacific coast from northern Peru to Trujillo, which predated the Incas by as much as 3,000 years. His particular interest was the Moche, who built the largest adobe structure—the Pyramid to the Sun—in the Western Hemisphere but today are best known for their ceramics, especially the portrait figures that you *know* were real people.

In the 1950s Larco bought a colonial vice-regal mansion in the Pueblo Libre neighborhood of Lima and moved the museum from Trujillo. By then the collection numbered 45,000 pieces and he stopped collecting, instead focusing on identifying, organizing, and educating Peruvians about their rich, complex, and largely unknown history.

Moche artifacts were the centerpiece when the Lima museum opened in 1956, although other civilizations and cultures were also represented. When the Larco underwent a major renovation and expansion in 2010, however, pieces from some of Peru's earliest cultures, like the Vicus and Cupisnique, were given space, as were the Incas.

Today the Larco presents its treasures in uncluttered, well-lit displays that take the visitor—in six languages—from the Vicus through the Nasca and Moche to the Huari and Incas. The collection emphasizes ceramics but textiles, jewelry, and body adornments—in gold, silver, and copper—attest to the extraordinary skill and creativity of these ancient peoples.

An exhibit of erotic art, next to the museum's café, leaves nothing to the imagination. These early people clearly had no reservations about expressing their sexuality. Heterosexual and homosexual couples are portrayed in intimate positions; even llamas and guinea pigs are shown doing what comes naturally.

And, rare for museums, visitors are allowed to prowl through the storage area where floor-to-ceiling shelves are packed with thousands of carefully identified objects. Among the treasures are Moche women figurines (there are none in the main museum), men who have been disfigured as punishment, people with congenital defects, dozens of animal and portrait ceramics, and pottery depicting everyday life.

The Museum Café offers a diverse, Peruvian cuisine with international dishes—a culinary respite that rivals the cultural treasures.

The museum and café are open daily to 22:00; the museum opens at 09:00, the café at 10:00. Both are easily accessible via long ramps. Admission: S/35; seniors S/30. Purchase tickets online at www.museolarco.org/tickets/, and choose one of four admission times: 10:00-12:00, 13:00-15:00; 15:00-17.00, and 17:00-19:00. A previously selected time is not required but there may be a wait if the museum is full. Av. Simón Bolívar 1515, Pueblo Libre, Lima.

Tel: (0051)461-1312 or 461-1835.

www.museolarco.org.

NOTES

Section 3: The Chimú

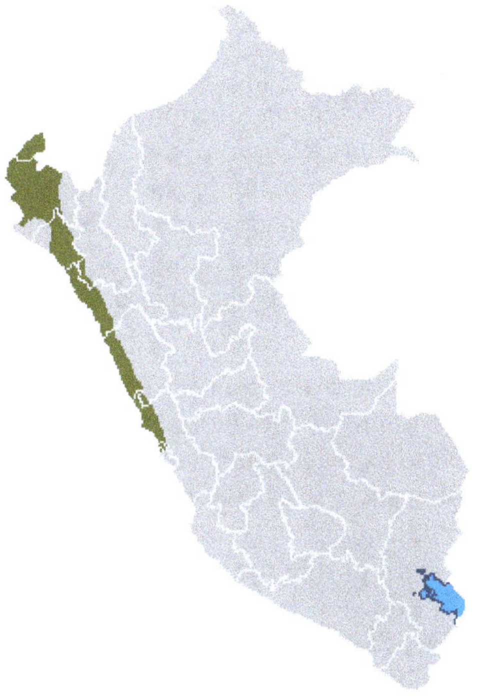

History

There are at least two Chimú creation myths. One is that the sun populated the world by creating three eggs: gold for the elite, silver for their wives, and copper for everyone else. The other myth is that two stars gave rise to the elites; two other stars gave rise to the common people. Both imply that there was sharp social stratification in Chimú society, and that this division was rooted in the cosmos. Indeed, the lowest social tier was fishermen; then farmers who lived further away; then artisans, craftsmen, and finally the rulers and their extended families who inhabited the palaces.

Another third story, perhaps rooted in reality, is that Chimú ancestors sailed down the coast from the north. A semi-mythical figure, *Tacaynamo*, founded the city of Chan Chan and was the first of 11 kings to govern Chimor (the empire's name). Indeed, recent studies have found evidence that migration from North to South America took place by sea before it happened overland.[15]

Chimor was born out of a shared world view. It began developing in the 10th century CE from the remnants of Moche culture, took two centuries to consolidate, and continued for half a millennium. There are continuities with the Moche, most notably irrigation systems and some art. Chimor encompassed all of that culture's geography and more. Along the coast, other cultures developed and it took the Chimú 100 years to conquer them.

In northern Peru near Ecuador the Tucume were a strategic target for the Chimú in the fourteenth century. The entire landscape is man-made; yet, after the initial invasion, there is no evidence of violence. Serra Chapolo is 250 km (155 mi) north of Chan Chan and 23 km (13 mi) north of Tucume; it was home to the Chimú elite sent to rule the northern region of the empire, although there is evidence that the Chimú shared power with the local elite—a practice the Incas would continue. Precious metals and shells have been found in the area along with 26 monumental pyramids.

A fortified site has been uncovered but it appears to have been defensive in character; the Chimú wanted to protect themselves from surprise attack. Graves near the site do not reveal violent deaths.

Over a century, Chimor's expansion increased the size of the empire bringing lucrative trade routes from the north and from the Andes under Chimú control. All wealth and abundance were channeled back to Chan Chan. At its height, Chimor was the largest pre-Inca political system in South America, extending

---

[15] Jason Daley, First Humans Entered the Americas along the Coast, Not Through the Ice. 11 Aug 2016. http://www.smithsonianmag.com/smart-news/humans-colonized-americas-along-coast-not-through-ice-180960103/

1,300 km (807 mi) north and south, from near the Ecuadorean border to near Lima.

In the 1460s Chimor was challenged by a civilization that would change western South America forever. Around 1463 the Incas descended from the mountains and laid claim to Chimor. In 1470, after seven years of struggle, the last of 11 known Chimú kings, Minchançaman, was defeated and exiled to Cusco. With no one in control the Chimú were lost. Chan Chan was abandoned and the people scattered throughout the desert.

Governance.

Chimor was the only empire before the Incas with a central administration. The center of a four-level hierarchy was at Chan Chan, with "provincial capitals" in other river valleys; subordinate centres that managed water, land, and labour, moved resources to Chan Chan, or implemented other administrative edicts; and villages. Rural sites were established as engineering headquarters during canal construction; when the canals were finished, they became maintenance centres.

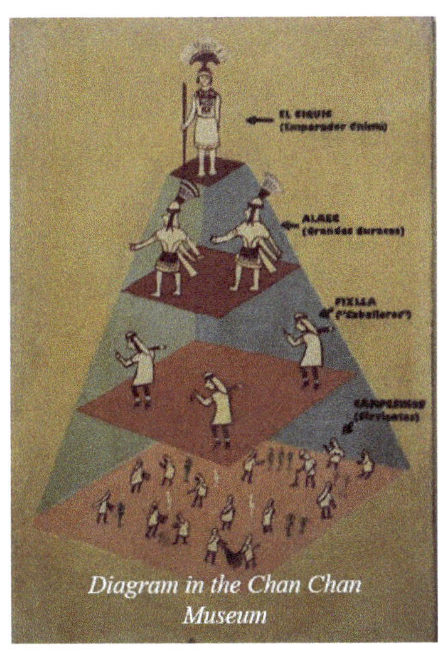

Diagram in the Chan Chan Museum

People paid tribute to the state with produce or labour; the surplus was stored for times of need, but it also fueled population growth and consolidated the power of state.

Agriculture. River valleys are key to understanding the rise of Chimor, as they have been elsewhere in the world. The deserts of northern Peru are real deserts; there are few plants or animals. Water runs through normally dry riverbeds with the spring thaw in the Andes beginning in January and then dries up by May. This pattern could be disrupted by El Niño, which periodically brought massive rainfall, widespread destruction, and reduced harvests from the sea.

Making the desert bloom required two things. One, both the Moche and the Chimú were forced to enrich the soil, which they did by transporting it from inland. Second, with enormous human effort, using only hand tools, they carved irrigation canals into the land.

These were not simple, linear irrigation ditches. Indeed, the engineering surpassed all previous efforts in the region. As hydraulic engineer Charles Ortloff notes, Chimor was the "first true engineering society in the New World," using engineering techniques unknown in North America and Europe until the nineteenth century.[16] The canals wound and turned in order to make the water flow slowly. There was an imperceptible, downhill gradient of 1:10,000. As the population, grew canals became larger and the Chimú controlled them. A network of canals connecting river valleys was developed.

It has been said that the Chimú had more acreage under cultivation in its empire—about 547 km² (340 mi²) of irrigated land—than modern Peru in the same coastal region. Around the Rio Moche alone, they grew maize, cotton, beans, and squash on over 20,000 hectares (almost 50,000 acres).

Religion. Like the Moche, the *Chimú* had a creator god, *Ai Apaec*, worshiped the moon (*Si*) and viewed the sun as a destroyer. They also worshiped the sea (*Ni*), whose anthropomorphized Wave Deity governed the sea and the moon—the two indomitable forces of the coastal environment. The Chimú believed the gods could whip up the ocean into storms and endow creatures with unearthly powers. To try and control the sea, offerings of white corn flour and other items

---

[17] Bruce Hathaway, Endangered Site: Chan Chan, Peru. March 2009. Smithsonian.com. http://www.smithsonianmag.com/travel/ endangered-site-chan-chan-peru-51748031/

were made. The pelican was a holy bird because it helped fishermen identify where fish were.

Another god, the Moon Animal, is found in both Moche and Chimú ceramics and was an important deity for at least 1,000 years. It is a four-legged figure with a crest and fangs; often it is depicted sitting or standing on a crescent moon, as if it is on a boat.

While little is known about Chimú religious practices, it is reasonable to assume that there were priests and shamans. Unlike other cultures, including the Moche and the Maya, Chimú drawings lack detail that allows priests to be identified.

There is strong evidence that offerings were a central part of religious practices. The *Spondylus* shell continued to be highly prized, was used in jewelry and other ornaments, but was most important as a symbol of the sea and rainfall. At various sites, large numbers of *Spondylus* shells have been uncovered, along with coca leaves, llamas, quartz crystals, the fermented corn drink, *chicha,* and human sacrifices.

While excavating a village near Chan Chan, archaeologists stumbled on the remains of 43 individuals, including boys and girls from 10 to 14 years of age. This was a mass sacrifice; ritual killing was evident in 50 percent of the remains. The sternum had been opened and the heart extracted. All the evidence provided a picture of how and why the children died. At some point the children, all healthy, were brought together in Chan Chan and were fed, while waiting for a special moment for the sacrifice. From an anthropological point of view, offering the best of a society was special and suggests that the Chimú were trying to control a very difficult situation. There is evidence of heavy rain before and after the sacrifice (in a region with usually little rain) so the question lingers: Were the children killed in an attempt to appease the god's wrath and restore normal weather patterns?

Chimú graves offer clear evidence of their belief in an afterlife. Young, sacrificed women, who may have been wives or concubines, accompanied kings to their graves. Among the more extraordinary Chimú artifacts discovered in recent years is a wood, three-dimensional representation of a royal funeral. Some paint is still visible and there are fish on the outside. Members of the royal family, priests, and a figure with his hands tied behind his back make up the procession. Another figure at the front carries a basket of *Spondylus* shells. Feathers surround the caskets; there is inlay of shells on the figurines. All are walking toward an adobe wall, like those at Chan Chan. Royals lived on forever in Chimú culture but commoners' burials, while lacking elite accoutrements, often included ornaments, weaving tools, cooking pots, food, and small copper pieces placed in the person's mouth. They too, were believed destined for an afterlife. In 2010 a late-middle aged woman was excavated with copper objects. Clutched in her right hand was a *Spondylus* shell—another indication that this represented the most valuable item within Chimú culture.

Culture. Inspired by their Moche predecessors, the Chimú continued to develop artistic motifs that became permanent features of Andean art. Using gold and silver from the Andes, amber and emeralds from Colombia, and *Spondylus* shells from Ecuador, their pottery, jewelry, and textiles reveal highly skilled artisans with a prodigious output who occupied a privileged place in Chimor. Some artisans were skilled wood workers; numerous wood sculptures, most of which represent funeral procession figures like that described above, have been found at two *huacas* a short distance from Chan Chan: The Rainbow Huaca (see No. 7, below) and Tacaynamo.

It is not surprising that artisans were rewarded for their skills. The artisan class had special privileges, married among themselves, and were buried in their own cemeteries. Artisans were allowed inside Chan Chan to work, but not to stay. When the Incas conquered Chimor in 1470, hundreds of artisans were forcibly relocated to Cusco, so highly did the Incas value their skills.

Architecture. The Chimú were master architects who created monumental buildings constructed entirely of adobe. In its time, Chan Chan was the largest adobe city in world, a monument to 35,000 to 60,000 people who lived there. Unlike other pre-Columbian cities, Chan Chan had no city centre, no central plaza. Instead, ten royal palaces, *ciudadelas,* built sequentially by Chimor's ten kings, were attached to each other and shared high, common walls designed to limit commoners' access. Inside, palace walls were lavishly decorated with relief designs featuring geometric shapes and animals, especially sea birds and fish. Low walls designed like fishnets separate rooms. The *ciudadelas* had as many as 15 U-shaped rooms with three walls, a raised floor, and often a courtyard. Their purpose was to control the flow of supplies from storerooms.

Outside the 10 m (31 ft) high palace walls, hundreds of smaller dwellings extended in all directions for several kilometers. Many were more modest adobe houses—homes and workshops of artisans and skilled workers—while most had a stone foundation with reed walls. There were also U-shaped courtyards and four *huacas*.

This architectural and urban design was repeated on a more modest scale at other Chimú sites throughout the empire, most notably Manchan and Farfán to the north.

Ceramics. Chimú pottery served two functions. There were pots, bowls, and vessels for daily use, and artistic ceramics for ceremonies. The latter features both moulded and shaped blackware and redware with sculpted decoration, which was often given a highly polished finish by rubbing with a previously polished rock. Decorations included land and maritime fauna, fruit, geometric designs, and deities.

Turkey vulture on left; sea lion on right.

Metallurgy. Metalworking rose to a high art in the late Chimú period. There were workshops with separate areas for gold, stamping, plating, pearl, and embossing wooden molds. A great variety of objects was produced: figurines, containers, knives, cups, bracelets, pins, crowns, and body plates. Gold and silver came from the high Andes; copper, found in small quantities along the coast, was a three-day walk away.

Silver and gold Moche head dress, earrings, nose ring, and necklace.
Larco Museum.

Textiles. Using backstrap looms, cotton, vicuña, llama, but primarily alpaca wool, the Chimú produced a great variety of textiles in natural colours, from plain weaves to patterned gauzes to brocades. Cloth was decorated with painting, feathers, embroidery, silver, and gold. The most popular designs featured figures with open arms and headdresses, probably rulers, double-headed snakes, and marine figures such as tuna and pelicans. One surviving tunic has 7,000 small gold squares individually sewn onto the fabric.

6. Chan Chan

Website: https://chanchan.gob.pe/

How to Get There

Chan Chan is located on the north side of Trujillo and abuts the city. Indeed, parts of Chan Chan are within Trujillo; see the Rainbow (Dragon) Pyramid (#5), below. One route, if you are outside Trujillo on the western side, is north on the Pan-American Highway for a few kilometers, then east on an access road that takes you through what was the residential areas of Chan Chan at its height. There are two options for visiting Chan Chan: take a tour, which can be arranged online ahead of time, or from your hotel in Trujillo; or, hire a local taxi driver to take you to the site and wait for you. There are always tourist taxis at the Plaza de Armas, identifiable because they are black and their drivers are always dressed in black pants and white dress shirts. At Chan Chan, you can hire a licenced guide.

If you have rented a car and are in Trujillo, take the Avenida España and Avenida Mansiche to Av. Huanchaco. This will take about 17 minutes. Turn left on Huanchaco and drive about two minutes to Chan Chan, on your left.

Visitor Information

Chan Chan is open from 09:00 to 16:00. Plan to spend at least 90 minutes here. The museum, which is located on Av. Mansiche about 500m before Av. Huanchaco, is open 09:00 to 17:00 every day except Monday. Admission is S/10 for adults, S/5 for secondary students, and S/1 for elementary school students.

Admission to Chan Chan is S/10 per person. A guide is strongly recommended because the signage around the site is limited. If you are pressed for time, you can do a 40-minute tour with a licenced guide that hits all the highlights. In September 2018, this cost US$40 for two people. There are fish-shaped pointers that will lead you through the site but a great deal of detail and history will be missed without a guide.

At the entrance, there are washrooms, a souvenir shop, and a kiosk with snacks.

Access: Chan Chan is the only archaeological site in the Trujillo area that is completely flat; therefore, visitors with mobility issues will have an easy time getting around.

Exploring the Site

Guardian Statue
Chan Chan Museum

At its height, Chan Chan was the largest city in the Western Hemisphere and the largest adobe city in the world. It covered an area of 15 km² (9 mi²) and had over 10,000 structures, many with walls almost 10 m (31 ft) high, that were stitched together via passageways and streets. Some of the interior walls, decorated with elaborate friezes, were several hundred meters long.

The ten royal palaces, constructed over the centuries, have rectangular layouts with double exterior walls, large interiors, only one entrance, and no enclosures open to the north. Located within each compound were administrative and storage buildings as well as burial platforms that contained the mummies of departed kings. In Chan Chan palaces housed the living and the dead; the palace in which the ruler had resided became their mausoleum.

The palaces grew larger over time; the McMansion of them all covers 220,000 m² (2,368,060 ft²). Storerooms also grew more numerous, evidence of Chimor's policy of collecting tribute from throughout the empire. There was an extensive irrigation system with canals, wells, and shallow reservoirs.

The reason for the multiple palaces was "split inheritance." When a king died, the next in line inherited the right to rule but not the wealth. As a result, each new king had to establish his own reputation and gather his own wealth—helped along by the system of tribute.

Entrance to Chan Chan is through one door in the wall. Inside you enter a long passageway that leads to the *Nik An* complex (previously Tschudi, named for a Swiss naturalist), which means "centre house". Here you will immediately see the centrality of water and the sea; the reliefs on the walls have fish pointing north and south, fish nets, waves, pelicans, and anzumitos (a now-extinct sea lion-otter). The north-south orientation of the fish may symbolize the two currents that have affected coastal Peru for millennia: the Humboldt Current, which flows from the south, and El Niño, which comes from the north.

Continuing through the site will take you to rooms with "fishnet" walls (below), the U-shaped rooms, large courtyards, and a reservoir. New areas of Chan Chan have opened to the public in recent years so allow two hours to tour the site.

7. Huaca Arcoiris

How to Get There

The Rainbow—or "Dragon"—Temple is located in Trujillo's La Esperanza district, about 4 km (2.4 mi) northwest of the Plaza de Armas. Buses to La Esperanza go northwest along the Pan-American Highway and can drop you off at the site. Alternatively, include it with a visit to Chan Chan or hire a taxi to take you to the site.

Tip: The Huaca Tacaynamo is five blocks southeast of the Huaca Arcoiris, with the entrance on Av. José Gabriel Condorcanqui between Santander on the north and Guadalupe Victoria on the south. It is another small Chimú pyramid, undergoing excavation, and may not be open to the public.

Visitor Information

Admission to the Rainbow Temple is included with a ticket to Chan Chan. However, we visited without going to Chan Chan and our guide walked us in.

This is a small site and a tour, including a stop in the tiny museum, will take about 45 minutes.

Access: The area surrounding the pyramid is flat and accessible to all; however, there are several stairs going to the upper level of the pyramid.

Exploring the Site

The pyramid is surrounded by a high wall, 60m by 54m (197 by 177 ft), and accessed through a gate. It has been beautifully excavated and restored so the art and architecture are clearly visible. Although it dates to the same era as Chan Chan, Arcoiris has completely different architecture and art. For example, there is no maritime iconography. "Rainbows" are the most common feature of the relief designs on the walls; however, below each rainbow is a pair of snakes. One snake has two heads and is holding a *tumi*, a ceremonial, half-moon shaped knife; the other's tail ends with a fish. At the top of the walls are dancers facing the entrance.

There are several lovely murals and some interesting "rooms" surrounding the pyramid that have no openings or doors. As many artifacts have been found in them, archaeologists believe offerings, including wood sculptures, were thrown into the rooms.

Section 4: Lima Culture

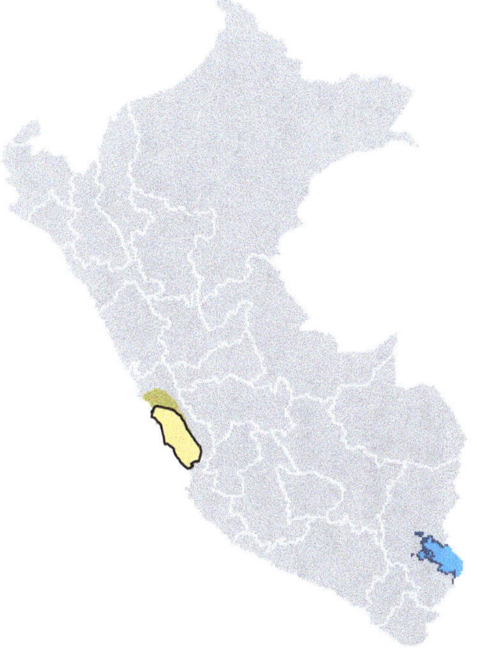

History

The Lima culture, which existed from about 100 CE to 700 CE, is difficult to define and differentiate from nearby cultures because of overlapping areas of influence and time. These factors plus the fact that many Lima culture sites have been overwhelmed by the growth of Peru's capital have contributed to the culture's obscurity. Both Moche and Huari (Wari) influence can be seen in its pottery, jewelry, architecture, and textiles. It also overlapped with the Nasca culture to the south.

The Lima culture built a number of ceremonial and administrative centres, including Huaca Pucllana and Huaca Huallamarca, but none would ever achieve the power and significance that Pachacamac acquired. At all these sites, however, the need for water led to extensive irrigation systems and terracing.

Four of these have been excavated, restored, and are open to the public: Pachacamac (30 minutes south of Lima near the coast); Huaca Pucllana (in Miraflores); Huaca Huallamarca (in San Isidro), and Cajamarquilla (in eastern Lima).

Lima Culture textile showing the Staff God. The Museum at Pachacamac

A Lima Culture Creation Story

All things emanated from Pachacamac, the giver of being to the world, an all-pervading spirit who gave plants and animals souls. The earth is "Pachamama" (earth mother).

In the beginning of the world when there was no food, Pachacamac created a man and a woman. The man died of hunger. Desperate, the woman pleaded to the Sun, father of Pachacamac, for fruits to sustain her. Instead, the Sun got her pregnant.

Jealous of this intervention, Pachacamac killed the son of the Sun and the woman, cutting him into little pieces. And corn grew from planting the teeth of the dead boy.

One day the woman, carrying the memory of her son, appealed to the sun for revenge. It re-created Vichama (her son), who then traveled the world. In his absence, Pachacamac killed his mother.

Vichama returned, resuscitated his mother, then chased Pachacamac who escaped by throwing himself into the sea.

—Ravines, Pachacamac

NOTES

8. Pachacamac

Website: http://pachacamac.perucultural.org.pe

How to Get There

Pachacamac is located 40 km. (24 mi) southeast of Lima in the Rio Lurín valley. The entrance is from the Pan-American Highway at km. 31 south.

There are numerous tours that depart from hotels in Miraflores and San Isidro. Arrangements for tours can be made online by visiting a Peruvian travel agency (such as the top-rated www.perutravel-vacations.com or http://www.fertur-travel.com/) or in the hotel. Alternatively, you can hire a driver for S/45-50 per hour (US$11-13) at any hotel who will not only deliver you to the site but will drive you around it and bring you back. This is highly recommended as tours are on a schedule and slow walkers or visitors who want to explore and soak up the ambiance will be frustrated by the hurry-up-we-have-to-leave syndrome.

From central Lima, minibuses signed "Pachacamac", depart every 15 minutes during daylight hours from Avenida 28 de Julio or the sunken roadway at the corner of Andahuaylas and Grau; the cost is S/3 (85¢) and is about an hour's ride. From Miraflores, take a bus on Avenida Benavides headed east to the Pan-American Highway and Puente Primavera; change here to the bus signed "Pachacamac/Lurín" (S/3 each). From both locations, tell the driver to let you off near *las ruinas* (the ruins). Otherwise, he will drop you in Pachacamac village, about a kilometer away from the entrance. To return to Lima, flag down any bus outside the entrance—and expect to stand.

Visitor Information

Pachacamac is open Tuesday to Saturday, 09:00 to 16:00, and Sunday, 09:00 to 15:00. Be sure to check availability on public holidays.

Admission is S/15 and includes the museum. Guides are available and many speak English.

It is the largest—by far—of all the sites in this book and, given its desert location with no shade, driving from point to point, then walking around each temple or area is the only sane way see everything in a reasonable amount of time, 2-3 hours. It is possible to walk but allow 3-4 hours to do it. Be sure to wear a hat and take water with you.

There is a visitors' centre at the entrance with a lovely museum that provides a terrific introduction to the site. A café and washrooms are available here—and only here.

Access: Much of Pachacamac is flat or on a slight grade. The only structure that requires climbing numerous stairs is the Temple of the Sun.

Exploring the site

Pachacamac, which means, "The One Who Animates the World", was the most important deity of later pre-Columbian coastal Peru. He was both the creator god and the god of fire and earthquakes. While the Lima culture founded Pachacamac around 200 CE, it would be occupied, developed, and expanded by the Huari, the Ischma, and the Incas.

The Lima people built the first temples using complex construction techniques that were unique for the time. Stone walls served as the foundation for structures made of *adobitos* (small adobe bricks), and can be seen at the *Conjunto de Adobitos*, near the entrance, the *Templo de Urpiwachak* and the *Templo Viejo*. During this period, Pachacamac's influence was local, but would expand dramatically in the following centuries.

The arrival of the Huari (AKA Wari) around 650 CE signaled the beginning of Pachacamac's growing influence. They enhanced and modified the complex but built only a few new structures, notably the *Templo Pachacamac*, also known as the *Templo Pintado* (Painted Temple). During excavations, archaeologists discovered many beautiful ceramics and textiles showing the Huari influence. They also identified a large cemetery. Even after the decline of the Huari, Pachacamac continued to grow and to increase the power, influence, and adoration of the god for which it was named.

Beginning around 1200 CE, the Ischma expanded the ceremonial center of Pachacamac by enlarging the *Templo Pintado*, then constructing 15 main temples and "stepped pyramids" with patios, ramps, and storage facilities. Adobe bricks and mortar were the primary construction materials, and the edifices were plastered but not painted. Two main streets connected the temples.

By the time the Incas arrived, around 1450 CE, Pachacamac's influence as a religious cult was so great that the Incas allowed it to co-exist along with their own sun god, Inti. They modified the existing structures, temples, and other buildings to suit their needs, then built new pyramids and temples, most notably the *Templo del Sol* (Temple of the Sun), which was constructed on a hill overlooking the Pacific Ocean and dedicated to Inti. The other notable Inca addition was the *Acllahuasi* (House of the Chosen Women), also known as *Mamacona*.

Tauri Chumpi Palace with southern Lima in distance.

Source: Instituto Nacional de Cultura, Perúhttp://www.limaeasy.com

A. Entrance and Museum

2. Adobe Complex

3. Pyramid with ramp No. 1

4. Street from northeast to southeast

5. Pyramidal temples with ramp

6. Second wall

7. Tauri-Chumpi Palace

8. Lurin Valley – Pachacamac

9. Casa de los Quipos channels

10. Residences and mausoleums and forest

11. Old Temple (Templo Viejo)

12. PachacamacTemple

13. MaxUhleCemetery

14. FirstWall

15. TempleoftheSun

16. Plaza of the Pilgrims

17. Urpi-Wachac Temple

18. Acllawasi

19. Puquios, cistern and

20. Urpi-Wachak Lagoon

9. Huaca Pucllana

Website: http://huacapucllanamiraflores.pe

Email: huacapucllana@miraflores.gob.pe

Phone: (+511) 617-7148 or 617-7138

How to Get There

Huaca Pucllana is located in the Miraflores district of Lima at Calle General Borgoño, cuadra 8. It is about eight blocks from the Parque Kennedy in the heart of Miraflores and every taxi driver knows its location.

Visitor Information

The site is open Wednesday to Monday from 09:00 to 17:00 and Wednesday to Sunday from 19:00 to 22:00. Closed on the following holidays: January 1; Good Friday; May 1; July 28, December 25, and national election days.

Daytime admission (until 17:00) is S/12. Children to age 12, high school and university students, and teachers are S/6; school children, S/1.

Nighttime admission (17:00-22:00) is S/15. Children to 12 and seniors: S/7.50. For security reasons, the evening tour does not include visiting the top of the Great Pyramid.

A guide is required for touring the site and is included in the entrance fee. English-speaking guides are always available although, if you arrive on your own—not part of a tour group— you may have to wait up to 15 minutes for the next English-language tour. If you want a private tour for your own group, which will go at the group's pace, it is an additional S/20. Tours in Portuguese, French, Italian, and Japanese can be arranged in advance. Send a query to huacapucllana@miraflores.gob.pe

Tours last from 45 to 75 minutes.

Tip: go early in the morning and you will likely get a more leisurely tour that allows time to wander a bit and to take photos. The 45-minute tour is rushed.

There is a small museum at the entrance, with artifacts from the site. There is also a large restaurant whose entrance is immediately adjacent to and overlooks the site.

Access: Most of the Huaca is flat and the paths easily accommodate walkers and wheelchairs; however, there are at least 25 steps up to the top of the Great Pyramid.

The Restaurant: Open 12:30 to 16:00 and 19:00 to 24:00. It is adjacent to the entrance and overlooks the site, which is illuminated at night.

Exploring the Site

The original *huaca*, which was built about 500 CE, extended well beyond the current walled site, and served as an important ceremonial and administrative center for the Lima Culture. There are seven staggered platforms and one large pyramid. Excavation began in 1981 and continues. The lower part of the site has been completely excavated along with about two-thirds of the great pyramid. Many of these sectors are open to the public.

There are two main sections. Section A includes the great pyramid and part of the northeast complex. Section B, also known as *Huaca Chica,* is separate from the rest of the complex and includes artifact examination rooms.

http://huacapucllanamiraflores.pe/visitas-plano/

A number of tombs have been uncovered at Pucllana, including warriors and priests. In 2010, archaeologists discovered four bundled mummies (*fardos*) from the Huari culture (800-1000 CE) near the top—6th platform—of the Great Pyramid. One was a woman of elite status; the other three were children who may have been sacrificed to accompany her in the afterlife. Five years later, excavations uncovered four tombs, three women and one man, from the Ischma period, 1000-1450 CE.

A one-room museum at the entrance (# 1 on the map) contains artifacts found at Pucllana. Behind the museum are three large holes in the wall. These were dug by Chinese immigrants for use as tombs (# 19) but were never used—unlike similar tombs found at Mateo Salado (No. 12).

From the entrance, the walkway leads past one side of the Great Pyramid, at the end of which a left turn takes you to the stairway leading to the top (#5), In one patio are many holes that were used for offerings (#9) and the tombs are identified. There is a 360° view of Miraflores and of the entire site. You may also see workmen excavating and preserving the outer side of the pyramid.

From the great pyramid, the path continues clockwise past a small zoo (# 11) with animals that would have been part of pre-Columbian life: ducks, guinea pigs (*cui*), and llamas. A garden (# 12) with typical foods is next and includes beans, corn, and squash.

The path continues past administrative offices, a residential and ceremonial areas (#'s 13-18). In the last segment, there are three re-creations of daily life (#'s 14, 15, 18) with life-size figures captured in a moment of labour or activity. From here it is a few meters walk to the exit.

10. Huallamarca

(AKA Wak'a Wallamarka or Pan de Azúcar—sugar loaf)

One side of the pyramid showing original (left) and reconstructed (right) walls.

How to Get There

Huallamarca is in the San Isidro district of Lima on Avenida Nicolas de Rivera 201 at the corner of Avenida El Rosario. Every taxi driver knows its location.

Visitor Information

Huallamarca is open from Tuesday to Saturday, 09:00-17:00.

Admission is S/5.00 for adults; children and students, S/1.00 and S/3.00 for university students. There is free parking.

This is a small site and can easily be visited in 45 minutes to an hour.

Access: The walking areas are flat and there are no stairs so it is easily accessible to all.

Exploring the Site

Huallamarca, the smallest of all the archaeological sites in Lima, is located in the middle of an upscale residential area. It is an adobe pyramid that has been beautifully restored but has left enough cleaned and unrestored that the building process is clearly visible. It was built by the Lima culture and dates to somewhere between 200 and 500 CE. There is a small **museum** just inside the entrance, complete with mummies and other artifacts that detail its excavation.

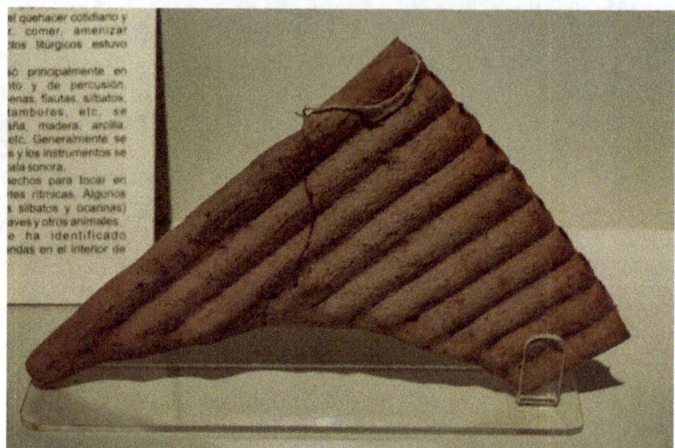

Clay pan pipe in the Huallamarca Museum

11. Cajamarquilla

Looking across the labyrinth.

How to Get There

Cajamarquilla is north of Purucucho and a 10-15 minute drive through lower-and working-class neighbourhoods. It is located about 30 km. from the centre of Lima in the Lurigancho-Chosica district. Taking a taxi, which can be combined with a visit to Purucucho, is the only option. Because the route is not marked and winds through residential areas, driving a rental car is not recommended.

Visitor Information

Because Cajamarquilla is undergoing extensive excavations, and has been for many years, there is no "entrance" or guides. We visited it after Purucucho and our guide was able to get us into the "labyrinth", described below. There is a large cemetery nearby but it is closed. Driving through the site, however, is interesting because one can see the streets of former residential areas, as well as the remains of many houses.

Access: The labyrinth is flat throughout. Some stage-like areas in large courtyards have 4-6 steps.

Exploring the Site

The labyrinth, at 167 hectares (413 acres), is the second largest urban complex constructed with adobe in pre-Columbian Peru, surpassed only by Chan Chan. Archaeologists believe that it was first settled by the Huari but was fully developed by the Lima Culture. There were streets, squares, pyramids, a cemetery, and the labyrinth.

Residential street just north of the labyrinth.

There is one entrance to the labyrinth, then follow your nose—or your guide—through what can best be described as a maze with myriad dead-end passageways, all leading to storerooms and some leading to courtyards with elevated platforms and the occasional *huanca*. There is a route that will take you to the far side of the labyrinth, via three or four courtyards and innumerable storerooms.

Allow 45 minutes to wander through the labyrinth.

Section 5: Ischma (Yschma) Culture

The Ischma migrated from the Lake Titicaca area and initially settled in the Lurín Valley south of Lima around 1100 CE following the breakup of the Huari Empire. The Ischma spoke Aymara, the language of southeastern Peru and Bolivia. Over time they moved north into the Rimac Valley, today the greater Lima area, building ceremonial centres a few kilometers east of the coast and on the far eastern edge of the city. They also inhabited Pachacamac, building new structures and remodeling others. The Ischma thrived until the arrival of the Incas around 1440 CE and were absorbed into Tawantinsuyu, the Inca Empire.

Burial wrap, Purucucho Museum.

NOTES

12. Mateo Salado

Photo by the author.

This is the newest archaeological site to be opened in Lima. The Ischma were relative newcomers; Huaca Pucllana was constructed 2,000 years ago by the Lima culture. Mateo Salado is named for a French immigrant who arrived in 1562, lived in the area, and was killed two years later by the Inquisition, possibly because he was Protestant.

It covers 17 hectares (42 acres) and has five pyramids. In 2009 the Peruvian government built a wall around the area to protect it; excavations began and the site opened to the public in 2014.

How to Get There

The site is located in the Pueblo Libre district with the entrance on Avenida Mariano H. Cornejo, between Calle (street) Enrique López Albujar and a large intersection with the Plaza a la Bandera (a round-about) on the southeast corner and Avenida Tingo María on the east side.

Buses: Any bus (and there are many) that travel north on Avenida Antonio José de Sucre—which runs NNE from the coast in the Magdalena del Mar district into Pueblo Libre, then changes name to Avenida Tingo María at the Plaza a la Bandera (a round-about)—will drop you within a block of the entrance. The major cross-street at Sucre, which runs from Callao (the port) to Avenida Brasil in San Isidro, is the Avenida La Marina.

Visitor Information

Mateo Salado is open Wednesday to Sunday, 09:00 to 16:00.

Admission is S/10.00 for adults; Students and children to age 12: S/1.00.

As this is fairly new newest archaeological site, amenities are limited; however, there are washrooms, benches, and a bit of shade.

Access: The main areas of the site are flat and one can see a good bit from the ground; however, climbing about 20 steps is required to access the top of the great pyramid (A), from which one walks across it and down the back. Pyramids B, C, and D can be seen from the top of Pyramid A but are not open to visitors.

Exploring the Site

From the entrance the path leads west toward Pyramid "E", the smallest of the pyramids in the complex and the most recent to be excavated (lower left on the map). Excavations in front of the pyramid revealed a road that continues along the west side of Pyramid A and that predates the Ischma but was extended by the Incas after their arrival in the mid-fifteenth century.

Pyramid E with the Inca Road running from left to right.

Pyramid E has several interesting features:

- There is a vertical line in the wall, which indicates a break in the continuity of its construction.
- Funeral wrappings were discovered, which indicates that it was a burial site for the elite.

U-shaped spaces in the wall are much more recent. Chinese immigrants, who began to arrive in the 1840s to work on farms as virtual indentured servants, were buried here in the 1940s. They weren't Catholic, so couldn't be buried in Catholic cemeteries and they couldn't afford to buy a plot in a secular cemetery.

Pyramid A is 20 m (65 ft) high and extends 5 m (16 ft) underground. It has suffered extensive damage by *huaqueros*—

grave robbers—and, before the protective fence was built in 2009, the pyramid was used as a bike ramp.

Our guide, Victor, described the pyramid as a "big onion" with 50 levels of construction and remodeling. The pyramid is accessed from the front via a wooden staircase and the view from the top affords a 360° view of the site and surrounding neighbourhoods. Like the Great Pyramid at Huaca Pucllana, there are several shallow holes in the top of the pyramid (left) that were used for offerings. From here you can see Pyramid D, which sits just northwest of the site, surrounded by houses; Pyramid C, due north, which has not been excavated; and Pyramid D, which has been undergoing extensive excavation.

Also visible from the top of Pyramid A and within the site are two farms that grew roses until it was discovered that irrigation was damaging the pyramids by soaking and softening the foundations. Now the families are negotiating with the state to buy them out, which should give them the money to relocate.

You leave Pyramid A by walking down the northeast corner, which offers a closer view of B and a close-up of A's eastern wall as you return to the entrance.

Original yellow paint, alcove, top of Pyramid A.

NOTES

13. Purucucho

The Purucucho Museum with outlying ruins on the hilltop.

How to Get There

Purucucho is located on a side road parallel to the Carretera Central East (Central Highway) about 25 km east of downtown Lima. Exit at km. 4.5 off the Carretera. It is a 25–40-minute drive from Miraflores, depending on traffic. Hiring a taxi to drive you to the site and wait for you is strongly recommended. While buses run along the Carretera, it will be a 10–15-minute walk to the entrance from the nearest bus stop. In addition, Purucucho sits on the edge of the Tupac Amaru shanty town, which simply means that this is a significantly less-developed area of Lima than the other districts previously described. A tour may be arranged through a Lima travel agency or your hotel; however, Purucucho is less frequently visited than the other sites so hiring a taxi is the easiest way to get there. You may also want to combine this with a visit to Cajamarquilla (No. 11).

Visitor information

Purucucho is open from 09:00 to 16:00, Tuesday through Sunday.

Admission is S/5 per person; university students, S/2; children under 12, S/1. A bilingual tour costs an additional S/20.

There is a lovely museum with wonderful artifacts found at the site, including items of daily life (sandals, fans, purses,  weaving boxes with spindles and yarn), ceremonial garb, and mummies. Washrooms are available here.

The site is a short walk away; however, if it is extremely hot, you may want to ask your driver to drive you and your guide there.

Access: Most of the site is either flat or accessed via ramps. There are a few steps (2-3) connecting some areas.

Exploring the Site

Purucucho means "feather hat" in Quechua. It was founded by the Ischma Culture, which developed in the Rimac and Lurín valleys between 900 and 1450 CE. When the Incas arrived, they built on what the Ischma had constructed, notably the small pyramids with ramps, which were used by llamas.

In the late 1450s CE, the Incas swept down to the coast and incorporated all of it into Tawantinsuyu, the Inca Empire. The "palace" at Purucucho became the seat of a *curaca*, the local governor, which served as both home and administrative centre(like Los Paradones, No.17). Nearby, there are a series of mausoleums built of rock that were discovered intact in the 1950s. Both the mummies and the artifacts buried with them are on display in the museum.

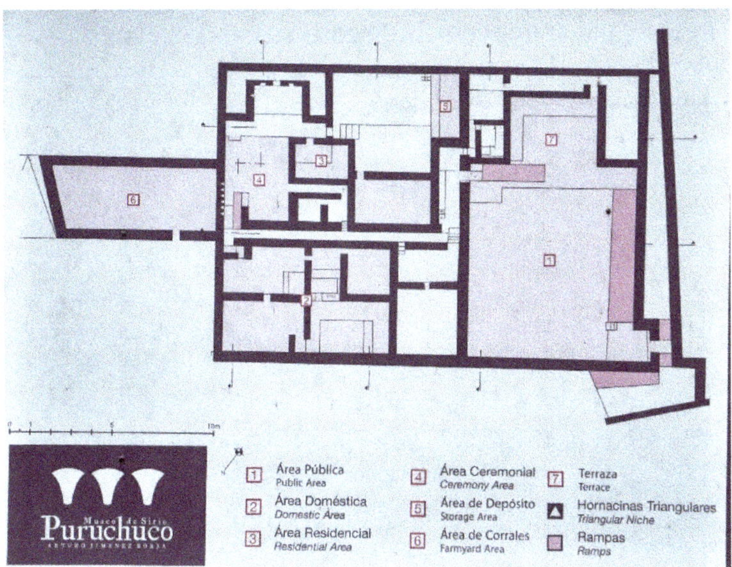

Map in the Museo de Purucucho. Photo by the author.

The palace has four areas and are accessed in the following order:

A. Public area, with a patio approached by a ramp, and a large platform with a U-shaped structure that opens toward the patio.

B. Residential area, including bedrooms and kitchen.

C: Ceremonial area, where religious rites were celebrated. There are six triangular niches in the wall, which are characteristically Inca and are the only ones found at any site in Lima.

D: Work and storage. This is a small area organized around a patio and a terrace. Initial food prep occurred here; two small deposits of maize and a *batán*—a stone used to grind grain—were found here in 2003, which confirmed its purpose.

Close to the palace are a series of mausoleums built with stones, first discovered in 1956 with their contents intact. Many of these artifacts, including the mummies, are in the Purucucho museum.

NOTES

Section 6: The Nasca

Map by Guillermo Romero (Huhsunqu)
https://en.wikipedia.org/wiki/Caral#/media/File:Peru_location_map.svg

History

In conversations and articles about pre-Columbian Peru, "Nasca" is usually followed by "lines" and that is the only the only thing most people associate with these otherwise mysterious people who inhabited the desert south of the Paracas Peninsula and a six-hour drive south of Lima. Nasca history and civilization, however, are rich and complex. They include innovations in ceramics, textiles, water management, agriculture, and recycling.

The earliest settlements appeared around 1100 BCE and grew slowly over the next 1,200 years. Between 400 BCE and 600 CE, the Nasca flourished in three river valleys, with Cahuachi and Ventilla the main ceremonial centres. They were among the smallest cultures in pre-Inca Peru; one estimate is that their population never exceeded 25,000. Still, at Cahuachi they

built the largest adobe city/ceremonial centre in history, 24 km²
(15 mi²), which received thousands of pilgrims from throughout
the Andean world. They were contemporary with, then outlasted
the Paracas Culture; indeed, many Nasca villages were built on
top of Paracas' settlements and there is clear evidence that the
Nasca used recycled garbage materials in construction. Indeed,
the Nasca may have been the first "green" culture in the Western
Hemisphere.

Governance was via chiefdoms that occasionally joined
together for mutual interest but were never a unified state.
Michael E. Moseley has written that "individuality—with
cultural coherence, but without large-scale or integrated
power—were Nasca hallmarks."[17]

Agriculture. Iconography on Nasca ceramics along with
excavated middens reveal a varied diet, which included corn,
sweet potato, squash, peanuts, *achira* (canna lily, whose root is
edible), manioc, and some seafood. They also cultivated cotton,
gourds, coca, and San Pedro cactus, the latter used as a
hallucinogen in ceremonies that have been portrayed on ceramic
bowls and pots.

The Nasca tamed the desert by developing *puquios*,
elaborate irrigation systems that tapped into water from the
Andes, and brought subterranean water to the surface, via
sloping wells that are still in use. *Puquios* minimize evaporation,
a critical feature in the desert. They planted seeds in single holes,
without plowing, which further minimized evaporation.

Ceramics. The Nasca's skills with ceramics are among the
most notable in pre-Columbian Peru. They were masters of
polychrome pottery and developed a technique of mixing as
many as 12 mineral pigments. The designs were baked into the
pottery, which has left their colours as vivid as the day they were
removed from the kiln.

---

[18]*The Incas and Their Ancestors: The Archaeology of Peru.* 1993. Thames & Hudson.

Textiles. Both cotton and wool from llamas, alpacas, and vicuña were used in weaving colourful and intricate designs. As these camelids cannot live in the desert, their wool is a clear indication of trade between the Nasca and Andean cultures. The Nasca often used figures in their designs, often in harvest scenes that show corn and beans. Animals, which are also found on pottery and among the lines, were also popular.

Metallurgy. Gold was the most popular metal and Nasca artisans produced full-face masks, nose and forehead ornaments, hair plumes, and masks that were worn over the mouth to give the wearer the appearance of having a gold beard. They beat gold into sheets, and then cut them into silhouettes.

Religion. What we know about Nasca cosmology is preserved in their ceramic designs and their burials. They used shaft burials, similar to but much deeper than the Colima culture in western Mexico. Nasca graves could be 4.5 m (15 ft) deep and a fair number have been found intact. The dead were mummified, usually placed in a seated position, and then wrapped in layers of textiles. There was little distinction between the burial of men and women; fine textiles and pottery were buried with both. Some have been found wearing headdresses made with the feathers of birds from the rainforest (the Peruvian Amazon), another indication that trade occurred across vast distances. Tombs were lined with adobe bricks and could be re-opened to add more mummies—a practice that may indicate ancestor worship.

What happened to the Nasca? In two words: climate change. Between 200 and 600 CE, the eastern edge of the desert crept 20 km (12 mi) inland and up to an altitude of 2,000 m (6,562 ft). Between 500 and 600 CE a severe drought caused massive disruption in agricultural patterns; Nasca society collapsed and, around 800 CE, the Huari supplanted the Nasca in this region, then remained for 300 years—until the Incas arrived in 1176 CE.

NOTES

14. The Nasca Lines

How to Get There and Visitor Information

The best way to view the Nasca lines is from the air. If you are driving on the Pan-American Highway between Ica and Nasca there is an elevated, covered observation tower that offers a view of the Hand and The Tree (above). This is a poor substitute for the views from a plane that flies at 1500 feet and circles each of 13 geoglyphs at a 45-degree angle, turning to the left, then to the right so that everyone on the plane has a great photo op. Closer to the city of Nasca there is another observation point accessed by scaling a low hill. Here you can see a number of lines and geometric shapes. (right)

Flights over the Nasca lines depart from Pisco, Ica, and Nasca. Nasca Flights (www.Nazcaflights.com) and Alas Peruanas (www.alasperuanas.com) operate from all three locations; Great Nasca Tours (www.greatNascatours.com) operates from the town of Nasca and offers tours from Lima.

As of December 2023, the cost for the trip on Nazca Flights, including 30-45 minutes flying over the lines, is:

LOCATION	PRICE (USD)	DURATION	HOURS
Pisco	$288 + $6 tax	90 minutes	Between 08:00-14:00
Ica	$235 +$10 tax	70 minutes	3 times/day
Nasca Lines only	$98 Tax inc	32 minutes	08:00-15:00
Nasca-- Includes Palpa geoglyphs	$214	55 minutes	08:00-15:00
Private, full-day tour from Lima	$360 per person	Includes 04:30 pick up at hotel, drive to Pisco, flight, lunch, return to hotel about 17:00	

The cost per person on Alas Peruanas is:

LOCATION	PRICE (USD)	DURATION	HOURS
Pisco	$290 + $4 tax	100 minutes	Between 08:00-14:00
Ica	$240 +$10 tax	60 minutes	
Nasca	$70 +$10 tax	35 minutes	08:00-15:00 On demand
From all three locations Alas Peruanas offers transfers to the airport from the local bus station, hotels, or their office.			
Package from Lima—15 hours	$449 Per person	Includes pick up at hotel, transport to bus station, tour of Paracas Peninsula and Ballestas Islands, flight, return to bus station, bus back to Lima.	

Great Nasca Tours offers a variety of one to four-day tours from Lima and Nasca, some of which include a flight over the Nasca lines. Check their website for details.

What Are the Lines?

In a word, geoglyphs.

They are giant, geometric forms etched into the surface of the desert. While the animal figures are the most famous, there are also innumerable straight lines and geometric figures, in particular trapezoids.

Why were they created? There are many theories. The most outlandish is in Erich Von Däniken's *Chariots of the Gods*, where he argued that mere mortals could not possibly have created the Nasca lines; they had to be created by extra-terrestrials. Apart from the lack of evidence, Däniken's argument is offensively Euro-centric and insulting to a culture that exhibited intelligence and creativity in manifold ways.

Other theories, grounded in scientific and archaeological research, have appeared over the years and have grown more sophisticated with new research and methodologies. In more or less chronological order they are:

- The lines were created for the gods to look upon them from above;

- They were a calendar with astronomical alignments to aid in planting and harvesting;

- They were not to be looked at, but to be walked upon as a sort of ceremonial procession;

- They are related to water sources;

- They were related to the worship of mountain deities that were closely connected to water.

The last two theories, which are not mutually exclusive, have held the greatest sway in recent years.

How did they do it? They cleared the surface of small stones darkened by desert varnish, exposing the lighter soil beneath. They may have used rope stretched between poles to ensure straight lines.

They were not made at one time, in one place, or for one purpose. Many lines are superimposed over earlier ones, something that is clearly evident from above. However, many can be seen from ground. Trapezoids and other geometric shapes are visible from several vantage points.

In sum, we know that the lines were places of social interaction.

Flying Over the Lines

If you are flying from Pisco or Ica, several minutes before reaching the most famous figures, the focus of the flight, you will begin to see lines and trapezoids. The co-pilot, who will be your guide, may say nothing about them; however, just before approaching the first of 12 to 14 figures, he will tell you what

you are about to see, depending on the flight and the company. They will include:

1. Whale (65 m long)
2. Triangles/Trapezoids(1-3 km)
3. Astronaut (35 m)
4. Monkey (90 m)
5. Dog (50 m)
6. Hummingbird (97 m)
7. Spider (46 m)
8. Condor (135 m)
9. Flamingo (300 m)
10. Parrot (65 m)
11. Hands (65 m)
12. Tree (65 m)
13. Lizard
14. Baby condor

"The Astronaut" (above right) is, according to one interpretation, more accurately "The Owl Man". The owl is nocturnal, uses its large eyes to see great distances and its ears to listen for predators. Carved into the side of a cliff, the man is looking to the sky.

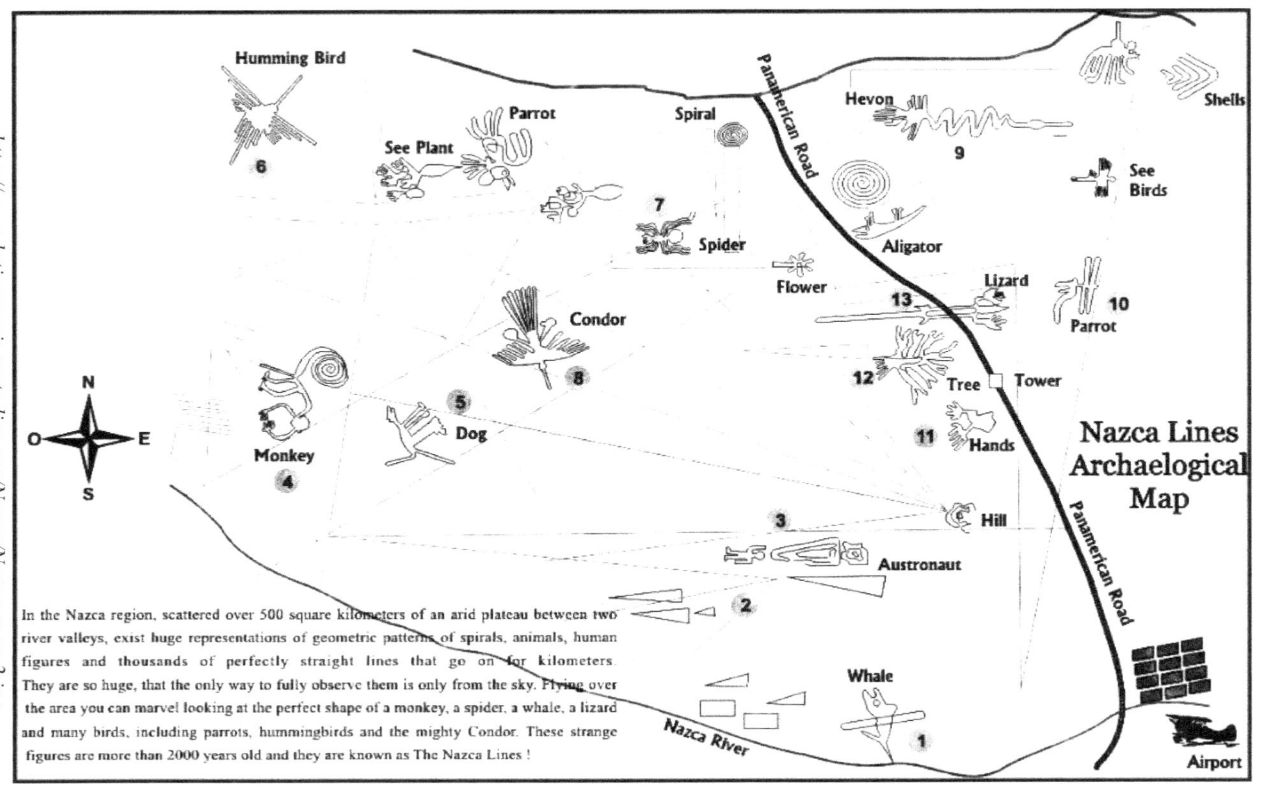

In the Nazca region, scattered over 500 square kilometers of an arid plateau between two river valleys, exist huge representations of geometric patterns of spirals, animals, human figures and thousands of perfectly straight lines that go on for kilometers. They are so huge, that the only way to fully observe them is only from the sky. Flying over the area you can marvel looking at the perfect shape of a monkey, a spider, a whale, a lizard and many birds, including parrots, hummingbirds and the mighty Condor. These strange figures are more than 2000 years old and they are known as The Nazca Lines !

http://www.latinamericanstudies.org/Nasca/Nasca-map-3.jpg

NOTES

The Maria Reiche Museum

"The Lady of the Lines"

Location: Km 421 Pan American Highway South, San José, Nasca Province.

Hours: 08:00-18:00, Monday-Sunday

Admission: S/5

Allow 45 minutes for your visit.

Mural, Nasca City.

Who was Maria Reiche?

Born in 1903 in Dresden, Germany, Reiche earned degrees in mathematics before traveling to Peru in 1932 for a job as governess and tutor to children of the German consulate in Lima. When World War II broke out in 1939, Reiche stayed in Peru and began teaching in Lima. A year later she began working with Paul Kosok, a historian from Long Island University in New York, who was studying ancient irrigation systems.

In 1941 Kosok noticed lines in the Nasca desert province that converged at the point of the Southern Hemisphere's winter solstice. He and Reiche began mapping and evaluating the lines for their relation to astronomical events. Reiche later found lines that converge at the summer solstice. Kosok left Peru in 1948 but Reiche continued the work. Two years earlier Reiche had begun mapping figures on the desert floor; ultimately, she would identify 18 different animals and birds. Her mathematics training helped her analyze the lines and led to her conclusion that they are highly sophisticated with great mathematical precision.

For the rest of her life, until her health declined in her 90s, she worked from her small house in San José. In the 1950s, she persuaded the Peruvian Air Force to help her make aerial photos of the lines, then spent years persuading the Peruvian government to protect them. Thanks to her efforts, the Nasca lines were declared a UNESCO World Heritage site in 1994. She died at 95 in 1998.

The Museum

Located on the east side of the Pan American Highway at km. 421 S, Reiche's former home is preserved as she lived in it for a half-century. There is a small museum with artifacts that she found during her research in the Nasca desert, all of her tools, her drawings of the lines, and her one-room abode/office. Reiche and her sister, Renate, who lived with her for many years, are buried next to the house.

One of the most interesting items in the museum is the mummy of a woman with tattoos, one of which is the *Chakana*, or Andean cross, on her right forearm. As noted earlier, the *Chakana* is found across cultures and millennia in the Andes.

15. Cahuachi

While Nasca civilization began to develop around 1100 BCE, it would be another 800 years before Cahuachi developed into the largest ceremonial centre in history covering an area of 24 km² (14.4 mi²). The first inhabitants migrated from Paracas and, as Cahuachi's fame and influence grew, thousands of pilgrims flocked to the site for ceremonies thanking the gods for water and waiting to hear the high priest, who was also considered a meteorologist.

At its height, there were 34 pyramids and 34 temples built entirely of adobe, with a vast plaza in front of the Great Pyramid that could hold 300,000 people. It was exclusively a ceremonial and administrative centre with no residential areas.

In the Nasca pantheon, the Wind God was the most important deity, followed by the Moon and Sun gods. There is evidence of sacrifices of llamas and birds but no human sacrifices have, to date, been found.

Cahuachi flourished for 700 years, between 300 BCE and 400 CE, thanks to the presence of water, then was abandoned over a short time in the wake of a super El Niño that brought an extended and devastating drought. The people, who for centuries had seen Cahuachi and its priests as their leaders and protectors, stopped believing in the power of the site and left, never to return.

About the Name

"Cahuachi" is not indigenous, much less Peruvian. It is, in fact, the name of a city in Japan (Kawachi), located between Nagasaki and Hiroshima. A Japanese immigrant to Peru purchased some land near the site and called it "Fondo Cahuachi", in honour of his hometown. Do not expect your guide to tell you this.

How to Get There

Cahuachi is 25 km and a one-hour ride east of Nasca city. You must go with a driver and guide as the road is not well-marked once you leave the highway and there are side roads that can take you in the wrong direction. The road is also not well  maintained so prepare for a bumpy ride. Soon after leaving the highway you will pass fields of cactus on which cochineal, the small insect that has provided red dye throughout the Americas for millennia, grows (right); a Minex Mine, and a Catholic cemetery.

Visitor Information

There is no infrastructure at Cahuachi, no washrooms, no reception centre, and only one Tourism Ministry representative. The signage is limited to identifying the major structures, so having a guide who can explain what you are seeing is essential.

Tour prices are variable. At the low end, a 3-site tour (Cahuachi, Cantalloc, and an Inca site, Los Paradones) with driver and English-speaking guide can cost as little as US$70 for two people, booked locally, but you will probably be in a group of 8-10. In January 2018, our guide and driver—arranged through a travel agency in Lima-- cost US$100 for the tour of

Cahuachi and it was worth every penny as our guide, Susie, was a walking encyclopedia of Nasca history and culture.

Susie offered sound advice for future visitors: Take the time before arriving to check out agencies on the internet and write them. The professionals will respond professionally and promptly. If you are arriving by bus, you will be met by tour guides eager to sell you their tour; do NOT take the first offer. If you have time, visit two or three agencies in Nasca city centre before choosing. Remember: You get what you pay for.

Access: Cahuachi is completely flat so visitors with mobility issues will have no difficulty negotiating the terrain.

A tour of Cahuachi will take 45 minutes to an hour, depending on how fast you walk and much history and detail you are interested in hearing.

Exploring the Site

The map on the next page is a depiction of what Cahuachi would have looked like at its peak. Today, all of these structures have been worn down by age, wind, and *huaqueros'* destruction. The path (116m/381 ft) from the parking lot) will bring you up the lower right of the map, and on your left will be the largely unexcavated oldest temple (350 BCE), which was destroyed by an earthquake. Then you will make a right turn and pass in front of the great pyramid on your left, which was the centre for public ceremonies. This pyramid was 40m (131 ft) high and had seven levels, the top three levels of which were reserved for priests and other officials. On the very top was an altar for sacrifices. Immediately after the Great Pyramid is a smaller temple, the *"Templete"*. This part of the walk is about 90m (295 ft).

To your right is a vast plaza that could hold 300,000 people for ceremonies. The Great Temple, which is directly underneath "de" on the map, was open only to priests and today is not accessible to visitors. After passing the pyramid, another right turn will take you past two more large structures. The first is the "*Pirámide Naranja*"—the Orange Pyramid; the second, near the end of the path, is the "*Templo Escalonado*—the stepped temple (below). This last long side, which takes you back to the parking lot via some low structures under excavation, is 213m (699 ft).

Along the way are signs in Spanish warning visitors to *not* stray from the path or pick up any ceramic fragments they may see. There are potsherds all over the ground and it is illegal to take them.

16. Cantalloc, Las Agujas, and El Telar

Cantalloc (AKA "Cantayoc"). When the super El Niño led to the collapse of Cahuachi, the people fled in search of water. They found it, near today's Nasca city. Cantalloc is one of 60 subterranean canals built by the Nasca between 400 and 700 CE, many of which, including Cantalloc, continue to irrigate fields.

This canal is 500m (1,640 ft)long, 150m (492 ft) of which is open. There is an imperceptible decline in the canals the water flow is regulated by small, hand-controlled dams or large rocks. At one point, two canals come together in a "Y" and continue flowing to their destination. The notable aspect of Cantalloc, however, are the 20 "windows", large spirals dug into the ground that, it is thought, funneled air drafts down to the water and kept it moving. Whatever their function, the spirals, which you can walk down, offer another example of inspired, pre-Columbian innovation and engineering.

Las Agujas and El Telar. These sites forcefully remind us that the "Nasca Lines" are not confined to the desert north of

Nasca city. In fact, they appear all over the southern Peruvian desert (which is a continuation of the Atacama Desert in Chile). The trapezoids, which are found from the northern part of the desert—flying from Pisco to the animal geoglyphs, they are the first lines one sees—to well south of Nasca, and particularly the "telar—weaving" geoglyphs will leave you impressed with the imagination and creativity of these people.

How to Get There

Cantalloc is located on the southeast side of Nasca city, just off the Carretera (Road) to Abancay and Cusco, AKA Carretera Interoceánica or Route 30A. From the city centre, take Route 1S (the Pan American Highway) south 1.5 km (1 mi) to Route 30A, turn left, and drive 3.5km (2 mi) to a side road on your left. There is a Cantalloc sign at this T-junction; turn left and go 400m (1/4 mi) to the entrance, on your right. Turn right, go about 140m to the welcome centre where you can park.

Las Agujas and **El Telar** are located just off 30A about 700m (1/2 mi) east of the turnoff to Cantalloc.

Visitor Information

For S/10 you can purchase a ticket that provides entrance to the four archaeological sites discussed in this chapter: Cantalloc, Telar, Las Agujas, and Los Paradones.

At the entrance to **Cantalloc** there is a welcome centre with at least one guide on duty. At **Las Agujas** there is no welcome centre and there may be a guide to check admission.

Access: Cantalloc is flat with easy access. Las Agujas and El Telar requires walking up a well-marked incline of about 25° to a small hill that overlooks the largest trapezoid and other lines.

Exploring the Sites

Cantalloc: From the parking area, opposite the welcome centre, you will see the above-ground canal and 16 "windows" just ahead. It is an easy walk around each window, the last of which is just before a reservoir; you can descend into all of the spirals down to the canal, which is up to 15m deep and a half-meter in diameter at the bottom. About 100m from the entrance, at the fourth window, to your left another row of three windows is visible and you can see where the two canals join at the bottom of this (4th) spiral. Allow 45 minutes for your visit.

Las Agujas (The Needles) The dominant feature from the hilltop overlook is a long trapezoid that stretches into the distance and seems to point to Cerro Blanco, the highest sand dune in the world. At 2,078m (6,718 ft), its peak is visible over the nearby mountains (Right).

El Telar, the "textile complex", is a collection of large geoglyphs, just east of Las Agujas, that represent several weaving implements including a threaded needle, several spirals that may represents coils of thread, and an area of squares that may represent a tapestry. These figures are not surprising, given that the Nasca were gifted weavers along with their many other skills.

Allow 30 minutes for your visit to the overlook at Las Agujas and to view the zig-zags, squares, and spirals of El Telar. From the parking area, it is a five-minute walk to the overlook where you can contemplate the meaning of the enormous trapezoid before you and the weaving geoglyphs to your left.

17. Los Paradones

Los Paradones is the only Inca site discussed in this guide and is included because it is close to the other sites discussed above and because it provides another chapter in the pre-Columbian history of this region. When the Incas arrived in 1476 CE and began the process of incorporating this area into Tawantinsuyu, as their empire was called, there was no complex of buildings that they could usurp and expand, as they did at Purucucho, east of Lima; they were forced to build an entire complex, now known as Los Paradones (the big walls).

How to Get There

Los Paradones is 2 km (1 mi) from the centre of Nasca city at the end of a wide street that begins as "Arica" in the city centre, becomes "Av. Los Paradones", and leads to a T-junction at Route 30A. The site is on the south side of 30A.

Visitor Information

For S/10 you can purchase a ticket that provides entrance to Los Paradones and the three archaeological sites discussed in Chapter 16: Cantalloc, Telar, and Las Agujas.

Access: Los Paradones has a well-marked path that ascends and descends a 100m (328 ft) hill with about a 35° incline.

Exploring the Site

Los Paradones is constructed of adobe, was built on a hill, and was an administrative centre with residences for senior officials—and a small *Acllahuasi* (House of the Chosen Women). There are also administrative buildings, warehouses, barracks, an observation tower, and a ceremonial area. As you follow the path up the hill, across the top, and down the other side, you will see potsherds and possibly remnants of cotton cloth lying around. Resist any temptation to pick them up; doing so is a crime.

Allow 45-60 minutes for your visit.

The following website has an interactive map showing the four sites discussed in this and the previous chapter: http://www.blogturismoinca.com/2015/01/nazca-atractivos-cercanos.htmlhttp://www.blogturismoinca.com/2015/01/ nazca-atractivos-cercanos.html.

NOTES

For Further Reading

Bourget, Steve and Kimberly L. Jones (eds). *The Art and Archaeology of the Moche: An Ancient Andean Society of the Peruvian North Coast.* Austin: University of Texas Press, 2020. utpress.utexas.edu

Gayoso-Rullier, H. *Huacas de Moche: Tourist Product, Interpretive Guide.* Trujillo, Perú: Universidad Nacional de Trujillo, 2014.

Jordan, R. F. *El Brujo: 5000 años de historia.* Lima, Perú: Fundación Weise, n.d.

______. El Brujo and the Lady of Cao: The Witch Archaeology Complex.http://www.go2peru.com/peru_guide-/trujillo/brujo_trujillo.htm

Lasaponara, R., Masini, N., & Orefici, G. *The Ancient Nasca World: New Insights from Science and Archaeology.* Springer International Publishing, 2016, doi: 10.1007/978-3-319-47052-8

Mann, Charles C., *1491.* New York, NY: Vintage Books, 2006.

Pardo, Celia and Jago Cooper. *Peru: A Journey in Time.* London: The British Museum, 2021.

Reiche, Maria, *Mystery on the Desert: A New Revelation of Ancient Peru.* 1949, reissued, Stuttgart: Stuttgart: Heinrich Fink Gmb,1968. (Out of print; available online)

Shady Solis, R. *The Sacred City of Caral-Supe: Cultural Symbol of Peru.* Lima, Perú: Instituto Nacional de Cultura, 2007.

Proulx, Donald A. "The Nasca Lines Project (1996-2000)".https://people.umass.edu/proulx/Nasca_Lines_ _Project.html

Useful Spanish Phrases for Shopping and Eating

All nouns are feminine or masculine. ("o" is masculine and uses the article "el"; "a" is feminine and uses the article "la". *Exception*: Greek-origin words such as map (el mapa).

BASIC PRONOUNCIATION RULES:

1. With few (important!) exceptions, Spanish is pronounced *exactly* as it is spelled.

2. The accent is almost *always* on the penultimate syllable, unless an accent appears elsewhere or a word ends in "l".

3. The "h" is *always* silent—unless it follows "c". "Ch" is a letter in the Spanish alphabet and is pronounced like the **ch** in **check** or **chess.**

4. "**Ll**" is pronounced the same as "y", so "llama" is yah-mah.

5. "**J**" sounds like "h" in English: "Javier" is HA-vee-air; José is hoe-SAY.

6. "V's" and "B's" are pronounced the same way and spelling is sometimes interchangeable.

§§§§§§§§§§§§§§§§§§§§§

GOOD MORNING: Buenos días (BWAY-nos DEE-ahs)

GOOD AFTERNOON (after 12:00): Buenas tardes (BWAY-nas TAR-des)

GOOD EVENING (after 6:00 p.m.): Buenas noches (BWAY-nahs NO-chess)

HELLO: Hola (OH-lah)

PLEASE: Por favor (pore fah-VOR)

THANK YOU: Gracias (GRA-see-ahs)

YES: ¡Sí! (See!)

NO: ¡No! (Noh!) (Both "sí" and "no" are usually followed by "gracias.") **HOW MUCH IS THIS?:** ¿Cuanto cuesta? (¿KWAN-toe QUES-tah?)

IT'S TOO MUCH/IT'S TOO EXPENSIVE: Es demasiado caro. (ESS deh-ma-SEE-AH-doh KAH-row)

WHAT IS YOUR BEST PRICE? ¿Cual es su mejor precio? (Kwal ess sue MEH-whore PRAY-see-oh?)

I'M JUST LOOKING: Estoy mirando. (Ess-TOY mi-RAHN-do.)

DO YOU ACCEPT CREDIT CARDS? ¿Acepta tarjetas de crédito? (Ak-CEPT-ta tar-HAY-tahs day CRE-dee-toe?

WHERE IS…? ¿Donde está …? (These words are contracted: ¿dond'está? – dohnd-ess-TAH?)

…THE WASHROOM/BATHROOM: el baño (ell BAHN-yo)

…A TELEPHONE: un teléfono (uhn teh-LEI-foh-noh)

…THE SHIP: el barco (el BAR-coe) OR el crucero (ell crew-SEHR-row)

…THE PORT/DOCK: el puerto (ell PWER-toe)

I WOULD LIKE….: Quisiera…. (Key-see-AIR-rah)

…A BEER: Una cerveza, por favor. (Ouh-na sir-VEZ-sah, pore FAH-vohr)

...**A GLASS OF WINE:** Una copa de vino blanco (*white)* or tinto (*red*) (UH-nah COE-pah deh VEE-noh BLAHN-coe *or* TEEN-toe.)

...**A PISCO SOUR:** Un Piece-coh sauer

...**A BOTTLE OF WATER:** Una botella de agua, por favor. (UH-nah bow-TAY-yuh deh AH-gwah….)

...**A COKE:** Una coca, por favor. (UH-nah KO-ka….)

...**THE MENU:** La carta *or* El menú (Lah CAR-tah *or* Ell meh-NU)

...**THE CHECK/BILL:** La cuenta, por favor. (Lah KWEN-tah…)

NUMBERS

1. UNO / UNA 2. DOS (doos)
3. TRES (trays) **4. CUATRO** (QWA-trow)
5. CINCO (SEEN-coh) **6. SEIS** (saze)
7. SIETE (see-ET-tay) **8. OCHO** (OH-cho)
9. NUEVE (new-EH-veh) **10. DÍEZ** (DEE-ehz)
11. ONCE (AWN-say)
12. DOCE (DOH-say)
13. TRECE (TRAY-say)
14. CATORCE (kah-TORE-say)
15. QUINCE (KEEN-say)
16. DIECISÉIS (dee-ez-EE-saze)
17. DIECISIETE (dee-ez-ee-see-ET-tay)
18. DIECIOCHO (dee-es-ee-OH-cho)
19. DIECINUEVE (dee-ez-ee-new-EH-veh)
20. VEINTE (bay-EN-tay)

COLOURS

WHITE blanco (BLHAN-ko)
BLACK negro (NEH-grow)
RED rojo (ROW-ho)
ORANGE naranja (nah-RAHN-ha)
YELLOW amarillo (ah-ma-REE-yo)
GREEN verde (VER-day)
BLUE azúl (ah-ZUL)
VIOLET morado (more-RAH-do)

About the Author

Tommie Sue Montgomery has been traveling, occasionally living and teaching, and doing research in Latin America since 1976. With a M.A. from Vanderbilt University and a Ph.D. from New York University, she has spent over four decades conducting research in El Salvador and is the author of three books and numerous articles on the country. She has also lived in Mexico, Belize, Nicaragua, and Argentina. Dr. Montgomery has received three Fulbright grants and, in 2013, was honoured by her alma mater, Wesleyan College in Georgia, for "distinguished achievement in a profession."

Since 2005 she has been presenting lectures on cruise ships from Vancouver to Cape Horn, up the Amazon, through the Caribbean, the Canadian Maritimes, and across the North Atlantic. In 2016 she published *Navigating Machu Picchu: A Short Guide to Planning and Getting the Most From Your Trip,* which was updated in 2019 and 2023.

When they are not traveling, she and her husband, David Abrahams, live in Oshawa, Ontario.

At El Brujo

NOTES